Bridge to Profit

Success Strategies of Today's Top Contractors

Bridge to Profit

Success Strategies of Today's Top Contractors

Eric Whitelaw

Bridge Media LLC
Edmonds, WA, USA

Bridge Media LLC
PO Box 1473
Edmonds, WA 98020

www.BridgeToProfit.com

ISBN 978-0-578-05125-3

Printed in the United States of America

CONTENTS

CONTENTS

Dedicated to my wife, Kaare; my bridge to happiness without whom I would be incomplete. Her patience, love and support have fueled my passion for winning in life and business since that fateful day she said "I do."

INTRODUCTION

"You are where you are and what you are because of yourself, nothing else. Nature is neutral. Nature doesn't care. If you do what other successful people do, you will enjoy the same results and rewards that they do. And if you don't, you won't."

-Brian Tracy

Most "how to" and success-oriented books are authored by men and women who have achieved a certain respected level of success in some area, whether related to business, sports, parenting, investing, or myriad other pursuits of life and work.

You might presume from the title of this book – ***Bridge to Profit: Success Strategies of Today's Top Contractors*** – that I, the author, am a top contractor. Let me state plainly from the onset that while I would be flattered, this is not the case.

Actually, I am a writer and a businessman, but the idea for ***Bridge to Profit*** is rooted in and was spawned by a longstanding connection to the industry.

I was raised around logging, farming and construction, and for the almost twenty years since college I have owned small construction businesses which have kept me connected to the industry. While my involvement has been limited, I have remained close enough to stay abreast of changes and advancements in the industry, and to make many keen observations.

I think the most consistent observation I've made is that for whatever reason, the construction industry is full of people who are really talented contractors, but apparently don't have – or know – what it takes to achieve success in the *business* of construction.

It is reported that almost a million businesses are started in the U.S. annually, and over 80% of them are belly-up or headed there fast within a year. The results for the construction industry, sadly, are fairly in line with this ratio (if not worse in some areas).

Through my research for this book, gathering information, data, opinions and anecdotal evidence, my hunch was repeatedly confirmed: the typical contractor is standing at the edge of a great crevasse looking across in desperation to the other side, which represents success and profitability in his business.

He's never had to cross a gap so wide and is ill-equipped to build a bridge, so either kills himself trying to build one from scratch, or makes the wise decision to take the much safer route of crossing one of the bridges upstream that have already been built.

I'm speaking metaphorically, of course. The "bridges" represent the successful business people who have skillfully navigated the tricky waters of the industry and already reached success and profitability. The gleaning of their experience and the adoption of their successful strategies can get you to the other side. You DO NOT need to build your own bridge!

This belief - that there are many contractors in today's market in need of genuine guidance and support - has led to the birth of this book and the Monthly Mentor Program. I am convinced that drawing on the success stories and strategies of actual owners in the business will consistently be of great value and benefit to many thousands of contractors.

This could ultimately benefit the public and even the economy as a whole, with industry standards raised and procedures improved. Higher standards lead to higher trust, an increase in business, and improved margins.

So, how do we tackle this opportunity? There are many ways, but I have chosen the old fashioned route: imitation.

I am a huge fan of innovation and creativity, whether it is the latest electronic techno-gadget or simply a new-fangled measuring tape, but when it comes to sales, business operations, personal development and other such generalities, I have always believed that it is rarely advisable to "reinvent the wheel."

Rather, the safest bet is usually to seek out someone who has successfully done what you want to do, and then copy them. In fact, the chances are excellent that any person you would deem worthy of copying achieved success largely through the successful emulation of others he identified as successful—however he defines success.

So, I went on a quest to find some of the best folks in the business; to pick their brains, and compile for you some of their best practices in a readable, usable and generally practical format.

In the pages that follow, you will hear their stories, be inspired by their triumphs and failures, vicariously experience their valuable and sometimes tough lessons, and glean insight and wisdom that no seminar, book or article could do justice.

What you will find is that the ideas found in this book will work for you no matter where you live, what your background or level of education is, regardless of your area(s) of expertise. Like the Champions you'll read about, it will be possible for you to take control of your life *and* your business, realizing your true potential and achieving the success you have longed for.

Now, please keep in mind that this is not a book that gets into the nuts and bolts of bidding, estimating, hiring, writing contracts, etc. While we do take some opportunities here and there to dive into tactical details, the goal of the book is to help you build the framework you will need to emulate success, capped off with solid examples and how-to's.

The book is broken into five parts as follows:

Part One | Pour the Foundation

This section goes into what is arguably the most important, powerful, unpredictable and dynamic element of your business that holds the key to releasing all of your potential: YOU.

Part Two | Frame it Up

Here is where you get to hear from the Champions, "straight from the horse's mouth." I pick their brains and glean all of the information – within reason – that I think you would want to get from these examples of success.

Part Three | Bring in the Specialists

When you are building a house, wouldn't you agree that no matter how beautiful it looks inside and out, it's virtually worthless if the toilets don't flush and lights don't work? The same applies to your business. Here we get to learn from a few of the folks who handle the technical and business aspects of the industry. Do not underestimate what you can learn from these folks.

Part Four | Finish Work

Now that structural and technical elements are covered, we dive into the quintessential elements of effectively marketing yourself and your business. Taking notes from the playbooks of Champions, you will ensure that you not only bring in quality business, but a steady stream of it for years to come.

Part Five | Sell It!

This is where the rubber hits the road. Equipped with a clear vision, a solid foundation, a finely tuned marketing plan and a cheering section of Raving Fans, there "ain't nothin' to it but to do it!"

At the end of each section you will find a TOOLBOX containing resources, recommendations and tips for applying the ideas and strategies about which you learned in the preceding section. The toolbox will be a great place to jot down notes as you will want to come back to these pages when you need to review or brush up.

Last but not least, be sure to read to the end of the book (but don't skip ahead!). Your optimism and confidence will fully bloom as you read the inspiring words shared by Chris Widener. Chris is an acclaimed author and motivator, and will have you jumping out of bed the next morning to go out and tackle the world. He's an expert at helping ordinary folks like you and me to become the best we can be—in our marriages, families, and yes, in our businesses.

Thank you for investing in Bridge to Profit. I hope that it will indeed be a bridge to the level of success that you deserve; that it will inspire you, motivate you, and most importantly equip you to go out and be excellent in your personal life, your family and your business.

Choose not to simply produce good work; that's a given. Build something meaningful, profitable and lasting.

You can... and you should.

p.s. Be sure to look into our Monthly Mentor Program after reading the book. See page 229 for more information.

INTRODUCTION

*"There is one quality which one must possess to win,
and that is definiteness of purpose, the knowledge
of what one wants, and a burning desire to possess it."*

-Napoleon Hill

PART ONE | "Pour the Foundation"

What's your "Why?"

W hat a terrific time to be in business. Sure, the economy is a challenge, the market is as competitive as ever, customers are educated and discriminating, and stress levels are high. But isn't that business as usual?

In the grander scheme of things, think about it: we live in the most prolific time in history and we have opportunities for growth and prosperity that are boundless.

There is arguably nothing that stands in the way of you or me being, doing or having virtually anything we can dream of. But something gets in the way.

Right now you might be thinking, "This all sounds fine, but what does it have to do with growing my contracting business?" Well, it really has *everything* to do with growing your business.

Have you ever thought, I mean deeply pondered on *why* you are in business? On the surface, the first thoughts that come to mind for most entrepreneurs (and do not ever forget that regardless of the size of your enterprise, you are an entrepreneur) are thoughts relating to money and freedom.

"I'm in business to make a living, with no cap on my earning potential." Or, "I like being my own boss and not having to answer to anyone." These are certainly benefits that come with owning your own business.

As difficult as it is, you must look within yourself and explore your own personal reasons for growing a business. I would submit that it ultimately boils down to our deep inner desire for meaning in our life and significance in our actions.

Do not discount the value—even necessity—of introspection. Ask yourself the following: What's important to me? What do I want to accomplish? What needs do I want to fulfill – both personally and professionally? What do I need to be, do or have to consider myself a success?

To help you get started, set aside ten minutes to take the Personal Objectives assessment below to rate the things that matter to you.

Be brutally honest (no one is going to see this, let alone grade it) and try not to think too long about your answers when taking the assessment. Think too long and there will be a strong urge to answer how you think you "should" answer. Answer quickly, and often you'll get the most accurate and honest answer.

For example, you may think that seeking recognition from peers or society might appear selfish or socially unacceptable. In actuality, some of history's greatest achievers and contributors to society were and are, among other things, driven by a thirst for recognition. If that is part of what makes you tick, don't ignore it, embrace it.

Take the assessment now. Circle the appropriate number from 1 to 10, with 1 being Relatively Unimportant, 5 being Moderately Important, and 10 being Very Important.

Entrepreneur's Personal Objectives

<u>Objective</u>:

To be creative   1 2 3 4 5 6 7 8 9 10

Personal achievement   1 2 3 4 5 6 7 8 9 10

Independence   1 2 3 4 5 6 7 8 9 10

Security   1 2 3 4 5 6 7 8 9 10

Meaningful work   1 2 3 4 5 6 7 8 9 10

Spiritual development   1 2 3 4 5 6 7 8 9 10

To make a lot of money   1 2 3 4 5 6 7 8 9 10

Recognition from peers   1 2 3 4 5 6 7 8 9 10

Recognition from society   1 2 3 4 5 6 7 8 9 10

Recognition from family   1 2 3 4 5 6 7 8 9 10

Time to myself   1 2 3 4 5 6 7 8 9 10

Time with family   1 2 3 4 5 6 7 8 9 10

Low amount of stress   1 2 3 4 5 6 7 8 9 10

Intellectual growth   1 2 3 4 5 6 7 8 9 10

Adventure and excitement   1 2 3 4 5 6 7 8 9 10

Strong friendships   1 2 3 4 5 6 7 8 9 10

Prestige   1 2 3 4 5 6 7 8 9 10

Opportunity to travel   1 2 3 4 5 6 7 8 9 10

To meet new people   1 2 3 4 5 6 7 8 9 10

To be a leader in my industry   1 2 3 4 5 6 7 8 9 10

Civic activities and politics   1 2 3 4 5 6 7 8 9 10

Attain Technical expertise	1 2 3 4 5 6 7 8 9 10
Having a stable environment	1 2 3 4 5 6 7 8 9 10
An affluent lifestyle	1 2 3 4 5 6 7 8 9 10
An active social life	1 2 3 4 5 6 7 8 9 10
Being attractive to others	1 2 3 4 5 6 7 8 9 10
Being liked by others	1 2 3 4 5 6 7 8 9 10
To have leisure time	1 2 3 4 5 6 7 8 9 10
To provide for retirement	1 2 3 4 5 6 7 8 9 10
To improve society	1 2 3 4 5 6 7 8 9 10

Take a few minutes to review your answers. Did this exercise reveal anything to you about yourself? If you were honest and objective, it most certainly did. If you didn't learn anything, it is possible that you are very in touch with your own drivers, but it's also possible that you might need to dig a little deeper.

The more knowledgeable you are about your own needs, wants, goals and interests, the better equipped you are to guide your life and business in a way that suits you. By knowing what is really important to you, it is much easier to seek out opportunities and avenues that will help you to reach your personal objectives and steer clear of those that won't.

For example, if you desire for your work to be meaningful, plan to do a couple of pro bono projects each year, fixing up an elder care facility or improving the playground equipment at a boys and girls club. If more time with family is important, devise a plan for empowering your employees (or hiring one, if necessary) and delegating more work. Perhaps you want to become a leader in the industry and make an impact that way; so set a goal to join and be active in one or two trade or community organizations.

The more you align your work life to reflect the things that matter most to you, the more fulfilled you will be, and ultimately you will position yourself and your business to be successful.

Look at your assessment often. With all the busyness of life, and the demands of finances, it is so easy to get lulled into doing work that really has little benefit beyond a paycheck. Don't get me wrong, the paycheck is important, and there are times when it is the *most* important.

But over time, you can succumb to focusing entirely on the revenue and drift into doing work that you don't enjoy, which really has no meaning or impact, and slowly kills your spirit.

What's *your* why? What truly motivates you? If you're not sure, that's okay. But you owe it to yourself to find out. If you identify it, and then shape your life and business around pursuing it, your life will be filled with more joy, peace and contentment than you can imagine.

Clarify Your Vision and Purpose

Zig Ziglar, one of the most influential authors, speakers and motivators of our time is famous for his powerful quotes and one-liners. These aren't just zingers that make great sound bites; they typically have some depth to them, even in their simplicity.

One of my favorites goes something like this: "If you aim for nothing, you will hit it every time." This is usually used in the context of goal setting, which we will get into in a later section, but I think it also fits in perfectly with the discussion of clarifying your vision and purpose in life.

Again, I implore you not to discount the importance of this section because it doesn't *appear* to fit directly into a discussion of how to grow a successful contracting business. If you take the time to pour the foundation properly, it doesn't guarantee that everything else will go perfectly from there on, but it certainly tilts the odds significantly in your favor.

In his classic <u>The Strangest Secret</u>, Earl Nightingale gave the example of a ship without a crew or map (if you haven't read or listened to this, I highly recommend it). If you simply aim the ship and shove it out to sea, it is nearly impossible for it to reach its destination. However, if you equip it with a map and an able captain and crew, it will reach its destination 9,999 times out of 10,000.

The same is true with your life. If you don't have a clearly defined destination in your mind, you'll simply drift at sea, never reaching anything or any place worthwhile.

You may not necessarily crash on the rocks, and you just might accidentally make a successful trip somewhere, but the chances are excellent that you will simply float about until the end of your life, without ever having fulfilled your major purpose because you failed to clarify it and plot a course to get there.

THE LIFE PLAN

One of the greatest exercises I ever experienced happened a number of years ago when I attended a three-day workshop out of state to help me develop my sales and public speaking skills. I was given the opportunity to participate in the professional coaching offered beyond the workshop, and to my surprise, one of the requirements was to write my life plan.

The thought of doing this overwhelmed me a bit, but the trainer gave me a framework to follow. It begins with a very unique mind shift: Fast forward to age 85 and look back on your life. Describe in detail what your life looks like "now" at 85, as a result of having lived your life the way you did.

In the pages that follow I am going to share with you my own personal life plan. To be honest, I debated for some time about whether to do this. It feels risky for a few reasons. First, I am a private person, and sharing something this intimate feels extremely awkward. Second, I risk scrutiny and judgment of my values from others by sharing them publicly.

Finally, I risk the potential embarrassment of failing at personal goals and objectives I have exposed, or the shame in occasionally displaying behaviors or qualities that run contrary to my stated values — God knows that I have failed countless times and am *far* from perfect.

That said, my heart and my own experience tells me that the value to you in seeing an actual example to follow in writing your own life plan far outweighs any negative consequences I might encounter personally.

So, in the following pages I will share my personal life plan.

Please use it as a guide to whatever extent you see fit, but don't limit yourself or feel in any way that mine is the only way.

The point is to go through the exercise of putting yourself at the other end of the journey, looking back. When you describe for yourself the life and legacy you want, and keep that in your mind at all times, it prompts you to live – every day and every minute – in harmony with that vision.

Will you fail sometimes to live in accordance with your vision? Many times! Sometimes daily! But, when you do get off course, you will know it, and you will know exactly how to get back on course. Without a clear vision of where you want to go, you could spend years, even a lifetime, getting farther and farther off course, and not even notice.

A final note about my life plan. You will see that my faith is a very big part of my life. My purpose is not to push my faith on you. If it makes you uncomfortable, I am sorry, it is not my intent. If it inspires you, fantastic. If it stirs something in your heart and you'd like to talk about it, feel free to shoot me an email.

Eric's Life Plan – Ahead to Age 85

Where do I live? *Kaare and I live in beautiful Edmonds, as we have for over 60 years. Aside from snowy weekend trips for skiing and snowmobiling, these days we spend the winter months in warmer climates, and summers at our cabin east of the mountains, where hundreds of wonderful memories have been created over the years with our family on long weekends, holidays, and summer vacations. Just like the day we moved to Edmonds, we still love to cuddle on the deck (regardless of the time of year), and watch the sun set over the Olympic Mountains and Puget Sound while recalling the wonderful memories of days and years past, as well as dreaming about those yet to be made.*

Who am I with? *I married Kaare 62 years ago, and I still think she's the most beautiful girl on earth. I knew when I met her that my life would be better because of her, that the children we'd have would be richly blessed with her as their mother. I also knew that she would be as good a friend and partner as I could ask for to spend my life with. I couldn't have been more right. We've had incredible highs, and some seemingly insurmountable lows, but one thing never changed ~ with Christ at the center, our marriage was a rock; one that could not be moved, broken or shaken. That rock is as solid today as the day we said our vows.*

What am I doing? *After all these years of what some might call land excavation, I am still spending time with my mistress, the wonderful game of golf. The ball doesn't fly nearly as far, but I still swing hard, just like I always did. In my middle years I got my handicap down into the low-single digits, and even broke 70 a couple of times. When I'm not golfing, which Kaare and I do a lot of together, we might be found boating, or at the cabin, or spending time with our kids and grandkids doing any of the above. Whatever time is left, I spend with friends or consulting with spiritual and business leaders, imparting the mistakes I made and lessons I learned on my many trips "around the block".*

What do I want? *I don't want for much, but to look back fondly on the years I spent here on earth, and to leave a legacy to my descendants. For all my successes, I had a lot of failures – and I'm thankful for both. I want to die knowing that I did my best to learn from them, and that I taught everyone I could how to avoid or at least improve upon them. I also want to know that I lived my life in earnest pursuit of fulfilling God's plan for me.*

How do I feel? *I feel peaceful. I have few regrets and a light heart. Physically I feel great, aside from some minor aches and pains from 85 years of working and playing hard. I tried my best to maintain a healthy lifestyle, and to that I owe the ability to still hit a golf ball and play catch with my grandkids; and after all these years I still take the stairs instead of the elevator when I can.*

What have my children become? *My children are balanced, spirit-filled, successful members of their communities. They have kids of their own, and are raising them to be productive, confident men and women. With God's grace and guidance in their lives, and Kaare and me as models, they learned how to have successful, solid and lasting marriages, as well as how to be loving, passionate parents and contributing members of society.*

When I am gone I want to be remembered as...
- *A man of his word, and one who was always there for someone in need. He could always be counted on, and derived great joy from helping others.*
- *A great father. His kids always knew that he loved them with all his heart, because he showed them and told them as often as he could. They also knew that he would lay down his life for them, and could always be relied upon to help them, teach them and guide them the best he could.*
- *A loving and faithful husband. Kaare was a lucky woman, he treated her like a princess. She could always rely on him to do the right thing, and she felt loved, supported and respected at all times.*
- *A spiritual leader both inside his home and out; one who loved God and shared that love with everyone he could. He also worked hard and long to lead others as best he could, with the hope of positively impacting the world.*
- *A business leader; one who achieved great success, but not at the expense of his health, family or integrity. He was blessed with high levels of stewardship, and richness and abundance of life.*

Epitaph:

He lived a life of purpose, and impacted the world.

Life Purpose

To positively impact the lives of all those I come in contact with, including my family, friends, business associates and clients.

Values
Spiritual
Marriage and Family
Finance
Physical
Vocational
Friendships

Clarifying Vision Statement: Spiritual

My life is devoted to God, and I enjoy the peace and richness of life that comes through a relationship with Him. I seek to be closer to God and understand His word.

Purpose: Spiritual

I seek to learn and understand God's word, that I may be a light that shines for all to see; to have a depth of understanding that allows me to lead others to a relationship with Christ.

Clarifying Vision Statement: Marriage & Family

My wife and children are confident and peaceful. They feel loved, respected, cherished and safe. They are happy and they enjoy life. I try to set a positive example in all areas of life, so that they may all grow spiritually, and live peacefully and abundantly.

Purpose: Marriage & Family

To love and cherish my wife and children, and to lead them in a loving and positive home. I spend quality time with them, developing bonds and experiences that cultivate faith, confidence and positive self-esteem.

Clarifying Vision Statement: Finance

Although my peace and security are not founded in the accumulation of money or riches, my dedication to proper stewardship has resulted in the release of great resources to us, and we have built substantial wealth. This allows us to impact the world in significant positive ways, and to provide a legacy for future generations.

Purpose: Finance

To build wealth, which can be leveraged and utilized to make a positive and lasting difference in the lives of my family, future generations, and the communities – both local and global – in which I live.

Clarifying Vision Statement: Physical Health & Fitness

I treat my physical body with respect. I resist temptation to eat and drink things in excess that are harmful, and that ultimately weaken my strength and spirit. I am strong and lean, my mind is clear and my energy is high.

Purpose: Physical Health & Fitness

To maintain the highest level of energy possible to devote quality time and effort to vocational, spiritual and family activities. Also to minimize any appearances, actions or habits that might weaken the example that I set for my family and others.

Clarifying Vision Statement: Vocational Excellence

I am a respected expert in my field, a consummate professional. I produce tremendous profit, and earn a high income for my family. I am very knowledgeable in my business roles, a trusted advisor to my customers and associates, and a leader and mentor to others.

Purpose: Vocational Excellence

To know that I am doing good work and bringing value to all I do. To develop and maintain the financial vehicles which will enable me to make the biggest impact on my family and others.

Clarifying Vision Statement: Friendships

I have many dear friends and lifelong relationships. I keep up with their lives and get together when possible. I stay involved in groups and clubs, and organize events and get-togethers. I also seek out and cultivate new friendships.

Purpose: Friendships

To make an impact in my friends' lives, making them feel loved and important. To show them my commitment to them, and experience their gratitude and affection.

I hope it was helpful to you to read my personal Life Plan. I humbly present it to you simply as an example. Whatever you put down on paper is good; there is no right or wrong thing to say or way to do it. The key is taking the time to write it down. And don't just go through the motions, make it real.

Finally, review it often. I do not review mine every day, but I do review it often enough to keep my vision fresh.

Be warned that often when you review it there is a little pain involved; the pain of conviction. Reviewing your Life Plan and being reminded of your true purpose and vision brings into light all of the areas where you are falling short. Trust me, the pain is worth it. Without the pain, there is no motivation to analyze your current location and take action to correct course. And when you don't know where you are, how can you possibly know how to get where you want to go?

Clarify your vision and purpose. Write it down. Review it often. Your life will reflect it, and you will experience the peace and success that you deserve and dream of.

Goal Setting 101

Setting specific, written and measurable goals is one of the most powerful action items you can ever do to become successful in life and business. Pick up virtually any book on success, or biography of a successful person, and without fail there is mention, if not significant credit, given to having *written, measurable goals.*

In the last section, we talked about clarifying your values, vision and purpose, which is prerequisite to setting and working on written goals.

The reason is simple: in order for you to be able to reach and maintain your goals, they need to be congruent with your core beliefs and values. For example, achieving a goal of losing thirty pounds is going to be very difficult if good physical health is not one of your core values.

So, with your vision and purpose in mind, begin thinking about the goals you can set to incrementally realize your vision. Following is a list of the areas in which you should set clear goals. Bear in mind that not every area will be important to you, but most should be.

Write down 5-10 goals for each area. When identifying and reviewing your goals, keep the following elements in mind. And don't forget, as Jim Rohn says, "Most people overestimate what they can do in one year, but underestimate what they can do in ten years."

1. Is it something you really want?
2. Is it believable or realistic?
3. Is it written down in clear and specific language?

4. Will you personally benefit from achieving this goal?
5. Have you set a specific deadline for this goal?
6. Have you set interim deadlines?
7. Have you identified obstacles in the way of achieving the goal?
8. Have you begun looking for helpful information and resources to help in achieving this goal? (This book is a great start!)
9. Have you identified people (family, friends, colleagues, mentors, etc.) who you can look to for help and support?

Personal Goals

Much happiness and fulfillment comes from external sources, like work, relationships, experiences and the like, but in order to truly enjoy them you must first work on the inside.

Family and Relationship Goals

Life is so much sweeter when your family unit is solid and relationships are stable.

Financial Goals

Zig Ziglar says "Money isn't everything, but it's right up there with oxygen!" It's true, happiness isn't all about money, but many things that do bring happiness are much more enjoyable – and accessible – when money isn't a worry.

Health and Fitness Goals

No one can deny the benefits of good health. It positively permeates every area of our life when our body is a finely tuned machine. You sleep better, you have more energy, you look better, your confidence is higher, and much more. Some areas to think about when setting health and fitness goals are:

- Weight
- Diet
- Exercise
- Rest and relaxation
- Nutrition
- Tobacco/Alcohol

Business Goals

This seems obvious, but let me ask you, do you have specific, written goals for your business? Or do you simply have an un-written goal to "make money"? If the latter, don't beat yourself up, you are part of the vast majority. Start now to set goals for your business and watch it grow.

Social and Giving Goals

One of the most important questions you can ask yourself is "What kind of difference do I want to make with my life?" Most successful people have a sense of destiny and purpose. They be-lieve they were put on this earth for a higher purpose and to do something that would benefit mankind. They have a passion about the rightness and goodness of their actions and are willing to make sacrifices to promote these ideals. In what area do you give back to your community or society at large? In what area would you like to leave a legacy? What are your social goals?

Education and Personal Development Goals

Success comes to those who are prepared to win. What knowl-edge, skills and habits do I need to develop to achieve success?

To help, ask yourself this question, "If I were the top person in my field (or hobby, sport, etc.), what skills and knowledge would I have?"

Now that you've written down 5-10 goals for each area, pull out the top ten goals combined out of all the areas. While all of your goals are important, these will be the most important. Write these on an index card or print them out, and put it up somewhere you will see it every day. Let your subconscious work for you as you become a radar-guided missile aimed at your goals.

There are literally hundreds of books and articles written on the subject of goal setting. While goal setting is critically important to the success of your business and thus important to cover in this book, it is not the main objective, so if you got some value out of the information provided above but would like to go deeper or get additional ideas, I encourage you to spend some time in the library and go through some of the resources you will find there. Or, if you are like me and prefer to own your books for future reference, jump on Amazon and click away.

I'd like to wrap up this Goals section with a quick story shared by Brian Tracy:

Mark McCormack, in his book *What They Don't Teach you at Harvard Business School* tells of a Harvard study conducted between 1979 and 1989. In 1979, the graduates of the MBA program at Harvard were asked, "Have you set clear, written goals for your future and made plans to accomplish them?" It turns out that only 3 percent of the graduates had written goals and plans. Thirteen percent had goals, but they were not in writing. Fully 84 percent had no specific goals at all, aside from getting out of school and enjoying the summer.

Ten years later, in 1989, the researchers interviewed the members of that class again. They found that the 13 percent who had goals that were not in writing were earning, on average, twice as much as the 84 percent of students who had no goals at all. But more surprisingly, they found that the 3 percent of graduates who had clear, written goals when they left Harvard were earning, on average, *ten times* as much as the other 97 percent of graduates *all together*. The only difference between the groups was the clarity of the goals they had for themselves when they graduated.

Which group would you like to be in?

Prepare for Excellence

W ould you competitively run a marathon tomorrow? Unless you are a long distance runner who has been training for months, the answer is a resounding NO.

If you disciplined yourself to follow a proven regimen for the next three to six months consisting of proper physical training, nutrition and mental preparation, could you competitively run a marathon? Absolutely. You might not place in the top five, but you could certainly finish it, and maybe even in the top ten or twenty percent.

Achieving real, not accidental success at anything requires

preparation. Sometimes the preparation is physical, sometimes it is mental, other times it is psychological. Often it is parts of all three, but almost all success, at anything, requires both mental and psychological preparation.

If you have decided that you want to be a successful – or *more* successful – contractor (and the fact that you are reading this book is sufficient evidence to support that) then you must take measures to prepare yourself for whatever level of success you desire.

Let's go back to the running example. For the average person to finish a marathon, months of training six days per week are required. That same person, however, may only need to run a few times a week for a couple of weeks in order to finish a 5K. The size of the goal and the starting point determine the amount of preparation required.

The same is true for the attainment of your personal and professional goals. Whatever your goals, some level of preparation will be required. If your goals are big and hairy, then you are going to need to do some serious analysis of your habits and actions to see that they are in alignment with what will be required to accomplish such lofty goals.

If your goals are only moderate in size and scope, then you will plan your actions accordingly. But do not be afraid to set big goals. Chris Widener says that we must set goals that are small enough to be achievable, but big enough to get us excited. We all have within us the ability to accomplish great things, if we will only set our sights on their attainment and take that first step.

Remember this when it comes to a goal: *You don't have to be excellent to get started, but you most certainly have to get started in order to be excellent.*

Daily Disciplines

Years ago a wise and successful mentor of mine introduced me to the concept of Daily Disciplines. The concept was not his own creation, but one he copied from a successful businessman he knew of (hmm, sound familiar?). He followed his own list of Daily Disciplines tailored to his life and business, and attributed much of his seven-figure income to this practice.

It is incredible how simple yet powerful this concept really is. It's founded on the old "Life is a trial by the mile, and it's hard by the yard, but it's a cinch by the inch." Or "How do you eat an elephant? One bite at a time."

In other words, when we break our goals down to very small habits and actions that we focus on every day, before you know it the goal is accomplished, and you don't get sidetracked, frustrated or discouraged by the size of the entire goal in front of you.

Here's how you can use it in your life and business. Let's say that you've decided that you want more referrals from realtors, specifically at least two or more per month. You estimate that you would probably need to talk to at least twenty realtors in order for two to give you a referral.

You could easily get discouraged by thinking "Where am I going to find the time to call twenty realtors? I hardly get any sleep as it is!" Alternatively, could you find the time to call just one realtor? Sure you could; there's always time to squeeze in a phone call. Do that every week day and in a month's time you have called 20 realtors.

There's a Daily Discipline. Do the above for a year, and

you've made contact with 240 realtors! I would venture a bet that if you actually did that, you would have so much business that you'd be faced with trying to figure out how to handle it all. What a problem to have!

Individually, you might want to lose twenty pounds. The thought of investing all the time and effort required to lose twenty pounds overwhelms you, and your calendar is pretty packed for the next few weeks, so you tell yourself that you will start that program next month. Next month rolls to the following month, and the next thing you know, you need to lose *thirty* pounds. Now it's even more overwhelming!

Create a couple of Daily Disciplines to take tiny, daily bites out of the elephant. One discipline might be to drink five glasses of water each day. Another could be to eat an apple every day. Soon you might add another to walk for twenty minutes at some point every day, or do fifty push-ups. Whatever, you get the picture.

Take a look at your most important goals and ask "What small tasks, if performed daily, would create my desired result?" It's easier than you might think to make the list. Hand write or print out a list of ten to twenty Daily Disciplines, and put little check boxes to the left of each item. Make a bunch of copies, and put them in a narrow 3-ring binder that doesn't take up much space but goes everywhere with you (this is a great place to keep a copy of your goals and life plan, too). Look at the list several times each day and check the boxes as each of the items are performed.

Don't beat yourself up if you don't hit them all every day, but resolve to try. Believe me, if you will incorporate the Daily Disciplines technique into your life and work, you will see incredible results. Eventually, the disciplines will become habit, and you can update the list with new ones.

"In truth, the only difference between those who have failed and those who have succeeded lies in the difference of their habits. Good habits are the key to all success. Bad habits are the unlocked door to failure. Thus, the first law I will obey, which precedes all others is—I will form good habits and become their slave."

-Og Mandino, The Greatest Salesman in the World

Be – Do – Have

I want to wrap up *Part One – Pour the Foundation* by presenting a very simple way for you to put all of this into perspective. Sometimes we get so caught up in the pursuit of what we want that we forget about the natural laws that are at work.

There are many natural laws, such as the Law of Belief, which states that whatever you believe with feeling or emotion becomes your reality.

While it might not be referred to as a law per se, Be-Do-Have is an irrefutable force. Simply stated: In order to HAVE the things or success you want in any area, you must DO the things necessary for their attainment. And in order to DO the things which bring success, you must BE a person capable and skilled in doing the things thus necessary to HAVE what you want.

If you will apply what you have learned in Part One, I guarantee that you will BE a person *more* than capable of the DOING, and you can subsequently HAVE anything you set your sights on.

TOOLBOX

- **www.BridgeToProfit.com** Stocked with tons of resources and ideas to help you efficiently and profitably run your business.
- For help in identifying your *Why*, developing your mental toughness, setting goals, getting motivated and many other areas of business and personal development, read anything you can get your hands on from these authors (in no particular order):

  - Chris Widener
  - Brian Tracy
  - Tony Robins
  - Zig Ziglar
  - Jim Rohn
  - Stephen Covey
  - John Maxwell

  - Steve Siebold
  - Jack Canfield
  - Napolean Hill
  - Tom Hopkins
  - Bob Proctor
  - Dennis Waitley
  - Michael Gerber

- Listen to the audio version of this book. Hear the actual recorded interviews and get the essence of the shared insight from the Champions themselves. The CD's can be ordered at the web site above.
- Enroll in the Monthly Mentor Program. See page 229.
- Feel free to email with any questions you may have. I will always do my best to reply within 48 hours. eric@bridgetoprofit.com

PART TWO | "Frame it Up"

Conversations with Champions

Here is the part of this book where we get to peek into the minds of contractors who have "been there, done that, got paid". These guys have established and proven themselves as leaders; the growth curve and success rate of their respective businesses reflect that.

My hope is that you fully appreciate the value of getting to hear and learn from these construction success stories. In an industry where it's "dog eat dog" and the sharing of success strategies is rare, this will be terrifically enlightening and refreshing.

As you read their words, take notes and re-read as necessary to fully digest what they have to say. Each of these men gave freely of their time to share their story, and did so purely with the hope of helping other contractors who aspire to be successful – or *more* successful – with their own construction business.

The men we'll hear from come from very different backgrounds, are different ages, focus on different areas of the business, and have companies of vastly different sizes and revenues.

Despite these differences they all share some common traits. As you read their stories you'll pick up on a few more commonalities, but across the board I observed consistently that they believe in themselves, they take their business very seriously and conduct it professionally, they are action oriented, they take measures to constantly improve themselves, and they are incredibly driven and persistent toward the accomplishment of their goals. Get ready to learn from some of the best.

Larry Sundquist
Founder and Principal
Sundquist Homes, Sundquist Family of Companies

About Larry

Larry Sundquist is a veteran of the construction industry, and one of its true success stories. He started his company in 1974, dabbling in many areas of construction, including fix and flips, new construction, land development, spec homes and more.

Sundquist has been a past Builder of the Year and is a member of the Home Builder Hall of Fame. These days, Sundquist focuses mainly on new homes and land development. This last year's production includes about 90 homes and total revenue upwards of $75 Million.

Larry has three grown children, and is passionate about public policy, missions, and spending time with family.

Author's note: I thoroughly enjoyed interviewing Larry, and I believe that you will benefit greatly from the thoughts, ideas and experiences he shares with us. Enjoy!

Eric: *Let's get started, Larry. Welcome, thank you so much for taking the time for us.*

Larry: Thanks, Eric.

Eric: *Larry, tell us about your background. Tell us about how and why you got started in construction.*

Larry: Well, it has always been a life-long dream to start something. My dad was a carpenter and worked with my grandfather when he was younger. My dad and my uncle had a construction company and built spec [speculative] houses back in the early 1950's, and it was just kind of a dream in large part from my grandfather to do something, even when we were in high school.

After high school, I tried a couple of quarters of college and that wasn't working for me, so I sold real estate for three years or so and doors started opening up that way. When I was 22 I started buying and selling houses and when I was 24 we turned this into a family owned business.

We started out buying a bunch of burned out houses, HUD Repo's. We added on and fixed them up. That led into spec building and land development.

Eric: *So, tell us about the land development side. Talk about the direction your company headed and where you personally like to be involved. What are your favorite parts of the business?*

Larry: I think very early on in our development we realized that we wanted to stay close in with our home building operation. There wasn't necessarily a lot of lots available [to buy and build on].

We very early on started developing our own lots. We didn't buy finished lots, we developed our own. In the very formative years of the company we started developing lots that we'd build on ourselves. After a few years, when we got into different economic cycles, when we started having a lot of inflation, it became highly advantageous to sell the lots because we'd sometimes make as much money selling the lots as we could building the house.

So, we went through cycles where we started actually selling many of the lots that we developed. In the mid-1980's we got to the point where we were more of a land developer than a home builder actually, and at that time it led us into building condominiums.

We started building condominiums up to four-story elevator buildings, but always maintaining a focus of developing lots that we sold to other builders. That's continued through today.

So there have been various periods of building condominiums, building houses, where one segment of the business was stronger than the other.

Probably four or five years ago we made a decision to really intentionally be a home builder and be very deliberate about it. We shifted to a path of trying to increase our single family detached home building operation, and started gearing our business that way.

That's a direction we've been headed which has been a little bit advantageous given the current business cycle because we already had plans to become a builder and it was all on lots that we developed ourselves, so we had a margin on those lots that allowed us to keep making money while prices were dropping, and burn up some of our lot supply.

As far as my greatest interests, they are probably in strategic planning and on the land developing side of the business. I hate to say it, but I've maybe gotten a little bit bored with building houses after building so many of them. It just kind of gets to be routine. I enjoy the planning part of it, and the strategic part of what we're doing and the marketing of it. But the actual sticks and stones part of it, I've actually grown to be a bit weary of.

Eric: *Are your homes employee built or do you subcontract?*

Larry: We subcontract virtually everything we can.

Eric: *Has it always been that way?*

Larry: Yes. I think from the very inception we did that. In the early years we did our own foundations and I've done virtually every thing that goes into a house except I've never put a heating system in. I've done plumbing, electrical, sheetrock, finish work; you name it, I've done it. I've done every bit of it along the way.

Eric: *It sounds like it was a very conscious decision to go the subcontractor route. How did you come to that conclusion? Was it simply to hand off those pieces and just be on the management side of it? What went into that?*

Larry: I think that it was to be able to manage the process, rather than letting the process manage us. We made a decision early on that we were not going to be a custom home builder, and we were not going to be building high priced houses. But our style of home building was to build production type houses and in order to build those that's what you need to do. You need to have a process that's managed, and if you're out doing the work yourself all the time, it ends up that the process manages you.

Eric: *On the subject of subcontractors: A lot of the folks reading this book* *are subcontractors and maybe want to keep it that way; they don't aspire to be a general contractor or developer or anything like that. Talk about the things that a subcontractor can and should do to help ensure a steady flow of work from General Contractors. In other words, as a GC, as a builder, what sorts of things are you looking for in subcontractors? What are some suggestions you can give to, say, a subcontractor who hasn't developed or established relationships with any GC's or builders yet?*

Larry: I think you hit on the key word when you say relationships, because I think that the key to success in this business—whether you're a home builder or general contractor or subcontractor—is relationships.

I think back to 35 years ago when I got started, how everything was done on a handshake. Occasionally you got into a "hydraulics contest" with someone but for the most part if you had a problem you worked it out and everything was done more or less on a handshake or maybe a simple one-page proposal from a subcontractor. Now we have an environment of suspicion and distrust and multi-page contracts and purchase orders, and a much more complicated system.

At the end of the day, with any of it when there's problems, things get worked out through relationships. I think that no matter what side of the business you're in, having good relationships with subs, vendors, etc., is a critical thing. Because you're always going to have problems, and you're going to correct those things through relationships. You're going to move forward with planning, whether it's trying to cut costs or anything, those things develop out of relationships.

I think it's a far better approach to have those relationships on pricing and bidding, than to constantly be going out and getting five bids and going with the lowest bidder, because you end up without those relationships.

Eric: *I'm sure after this many years, you have some subcontractors that you really prefer to work with. You perhaps even have some that you have been working with for many years, because they built trust and relationship with you. But, how high are those barriers to entry? If I'm a cabinet maker, painter, or what have you, and I want to get a shot, a foot in the door, with a home builder or GC, how tough is it to get in? And what advice do you give to someone trying to get that shot?*

Larry: Well, I think that those barriers can get pretty high, and especially in a company like ours where we have multiple levels of management. These days it's so easy to hide behind voicemail and e-mails. I'm a big believer in verbal communication, so e-mails are easy to delete and voicemails are easy to delete and trying to find the opportunity to have verbal discussions to sell yourself is hard. Also, it's important to be able to have a reference, somebody who will speak well of you.

Eric: *Right. Basically to give some confirmation to what you're saying you can do, to get some testimonials and get some work.*

Larry: If we're going to spend time talking to somebody, and that's kind of the way we get so we look at them some of the time, we want to know that we're not wasting our time, that there's some good fruit that can come out of it. Everybody in this industry gets very busy so you don't want to have meetings and phone calls that aren't going to go anywhere.

Eric: *So, on the other side of the business, if you're not a subcontractor but say a builder or general contractor and maybe a smaller one that is just getting started or has achieved a little bit of success but would really like to grow it, can you talk about your observations over the years? What sets a successful builder or GC apart from those that by far are the majority, who continually struggle and go from project to project and never seem to really be able to get ahead?*

Larry: I think the number one thing is to understand the basics of financial statements, balance sheets and really just making a profit.

I think for a long period in my career, I never took the time to do that. We were making money and I had money to spend and I think, frankly, I was probably 36 or 37 years old, been in the business for 12 or 14 years and one day I woke up thinking about what I wanted to be when I grow up. I thought about it and prayed about it and realized, "Hey, I am grown up and this is what I am".

It was purposeful and I loved what I was doing and we were making money and it was just a great experience, but I wasn't investing myself in understanding the business aspects of the business and I think that's a really key piece of this, whether you're a spec home builder or land developer.

The number two thing, if I had it to do over again, and I've counseled people on this over the years, is don't try to go for it all at once. It's too easy, the way it's been the last few years, to get so over leveraged and get in trouble.

I'm not just referring to this current business cycle where everybody ended up being over leveraged, but in past business cycles where people weren't nearly as leveraged as they have been.

The closer you can get to operating debt free, the better. I think starting off smaller and moving slower and becoming better capitalized and keeping down the amount of leverage you have is a far better approach.

Eric: *And if you do that, you probably sleep a lot better at night.*

Larry: Well I sure would be right now.

Eric: *Before we jump off this last topic, I think that's really great what you just shared. I agree with you that it's tremendously important that a person invest in themselves and become a student of running the successful business by understanding those financials and really knowing what's happening inside their business and where things are going.*

The majority of contractors out there are much like you probably were in the first ten years – if there's a surplus in the account and I can pay myself, things are going great! You can go through those feast or famine times. So, d you have any concrete advice for somebody to get themselves educated? Was it just the school of hard knocks for you or were there specific things that helped you do that?

Larry: Certainly the school of hard knocks is a great teacher, but I think there are plenty of opportunities to learn without having to suffer some of those hard knocks.

I'm a real believer in higher education and I'm also a believer that you don't need to have an MBA to be successful in this business. This country is great place for hard working people with an entrepreneurial spirit to get out there and do something.

I think that basic things, like classes at the community college level without the idea of a degree are great. The homebuilding industry has numerous seminars available on different subjects that you can study and learn about different aspects of the business. I think that a person availing themselves to those opportunities early on in their careers is an important thing.

Learning is a lifelong process and the world and the technology of doing everything is the main thing and you need to keep abreast of those things. There's a tremendous amount of opportunity for education out there and I think you need to find the ones that are appropriate for what you're doing and take advantage of them.

Eric: *Let's switch gears momentarily to marketing. There are obviously certain marketing strategies that are important for a company like yours where you have these communities that you're selling and so there's a lot of traditional marketing, I'm assuming. Some of the traditional advertising avenues are used, and you've got a beautifully done website which I think these days is important for just about any business large or small.*

Talk about some of the ways you've found to be most effective in marketing your type of business, but also for the GC that might not necessarily need to do a lot of traditional marketing but needs some of those key relationships with architects or designers, etc.

Larry: It's really hard for me to speak to the general contractor side of it because I know a lot of that is relying on the relationship to architects and to get leads on jobs it has to get done that way.

For us, on the home building side after 35 years, the best and shortest answer is "Do it yourself". I'm not talking about me as the principal doing it but having your marketing done in-house so that your people handling the marketing understand the philosophy of the company. They understand the product and they understand the market you're dealing with.

We've been, in one form or another, doing our own marketing for the last 25 years and the last probably ten years, our marketing is 100% in-house. We use outside companies to do the website, but we're designing it and they're implementing it. Our ads are also produced in-house.

Everything we do with sales and marketing is centered on what we do and that requires getting to a certain size before you can do that.

I think that an owner has to be directly involved and understand marketing to understand all of those components of what your product is, who your buyer is, the location of what you're selling. All of those things are critical.

You can't ignore marketing and you can't just zip it off to a real estate agent or some marketing firm. You've got to be intimately involved in it. For us this model has worked very well. One way or another, most of the larger homebuilders handle their sales and marketing this way.

Eric: *One of the last topics I want to cover with you, Larry, is on the personal development side. One of the missions of this book is to help folks become the kind of person that can be an effective business person and leader, and have a fulfilling, rewarding career that has a positive impact on the folks that work with them and for them, and on their customers and community.*

You've been in a leadership position for many years now, both as an employer and in different organizations that you've been involved in. Talk about some of the disciplines that you have followed to develop yourself as a leader and some of the ways that you think would be helpful to folks reading this, whether it's a mindset, or specific things they can do to be developing themselves in that way.

Larry: Boy, that's a tough one. It seems like some of those things just happen. Here in our company we have some very strong stewardship statements in terms of the way we function, in terms of the way we treat each other, the way we treat our vendors, the way we treat our customers and the way we interact in our community.

We try and abide by those things. We want to say that we're a company that's full of integrity. I honestly think that we've developed a reputation for that in the community.

We've been engaged in all kinds of organizations. We give charitably to the community. We sponsor community events and those things I think people respect, and all of a sudden they start making you a community leader for that.

You can become a leader through involvement in politics or public policy. All of a sudden people know you when you're engaged in doing things and you become a leader.

Sometimes people follow you and want to be part of what you're doing because they like you and sometimes it's because they hear you. I think that in everything we've done we've tried to listen to people. We have opinions, especially when it comes to issues of integrity and doing what's right. We're always going to stand up for those, but we try to listen to people and what they want and not be too bullheaded about how we approach things.

Whether it's dealing with homebuilding activities, community activities, with involvement in public policy organizations, involvement in church organizations, that's really how I've tried to approach things. Where I don't have patience with people is when they're not doing things the completely honest way.

Eric: *Have there been any things that you've been involved in, that intended or not, helped you develop some of these leadership qualities?*

Larry: I have never pursued any of the types of organizations that are networking organizations, per se, or done something like Toast Masters. I've just jumped into organizations and I think the earliest organizations that I got involved with were the home-builder organizations. I just jumped in and started doing things.

It started when we were having problems with city government and we started going to meetings. That led to involvement in the homebuilders association, which led to the involvement as the legislative chairman for the state homebuilder's association, which led me into roles with other business organizations in the state.

There wasn't really anyone mentoring me, I was just in the process of doing things. As I started getting a little older, and the kids were getting older, and I was realizing this wasn't really all about making money, I started getting involved in our church and some of the same things happened there. I started getting involved in missions organizations and some of the same types of things happened there, and then my interest in politics led to public policy issues that were involving the social fabric of the country. I can't say I've ever had anyone mentoring me, it all just happened along the way.

Eric: *Sometimes when you just step in and get in the fray, things just happen.*

Larry: I think [it's about] being available. There's a balance there. You can destroy your family if you get too involved. We have an organization that we're involved with right now and we have a board member whose marriage is in trouble because he's been involved in so many good things.

There needs to be a balance between the things you're involved with and your family. I think getting involved when you see a need and pitching in and being a part of it just kind of leads to that leadership that we need. Society needs that at all different levels.

Eric: *Without a doubt. Well Larry, as we wrap up here, if you could, please summarize some nuggets of wisdom from your years of experience for those who do aspire to grow as a person, as a business owner and to grow their companies. If you could just bullet off a few of the things that you would leave in summary, what would they be?*

Larry: Work hard. Persevere. Understand the economics of what you're doing. Continue your education. Be engaged in the marketing of whatever you're trying to do.

Eric: *Wise words. Larry, thank you so much. We're so grateful for you taking the time here. Sundquisthomes.com is the website for the Sundquist Family of Companies. A beautifully done website and it's an absolutely wonderful company. If you want to copy a home builder, this would be a good one to follow. Larry, thank you again.*

Larry: Thank you, Eric.

Charlie Anderson
Owner and President
Anderson Construction Group

About Charlie

C harlie Anderson is the President and Owner of Seattle-based construction company Anderson Construction Group. With a Business degree and a background in the real estate development industry overseeing the development of office, apartment and condominium projects throughout the Northwest, Charlie founded ACG in 2002.

As the President of ACG, Charlie manages select projects while focusing on the future growth and strength of the company and its ambitious direction. Since 2002 Charlie has led the company on a path of expansion through two outgrown office moves and the hiring of many employees, landing ACG as one of the fastest growing private companies in the Northwest.

Charlie and his wife have three children, and when he's not working, you can find him out on a golf course, rain or shine.

Eric: *Welcome Charlie, thank you for joining us.*

Charlie: Thank you.

Eric: *Let's jump right into it, Charlie. Why don't you tell us a bit about your background and how you came up through the ranks before construction and how you got into it, bringing us up to the present.*

Charlie: Well, I kind of took a unique route into the construction business. I was a finance major at the UW and came out of school thinking that I wanted a career in real estate development, and at the time, a 22 year old with really no hands on experience in the construction and real estate market, that was a tough job to get.

So my first job was at Arthur Anderson working in their construction litigation department and in my mind that was close enough to real estate and construction that I felt that it was applicable.

So starting with that as my experience I looked at large construction projects and issues that they have, and how those projects end up going down the litigation path.

Ultimately after a couple years I was lucky enough to get a job working for a large publicly traded company that moved from Canada and started a U.S. headquarters, and I knew some folks there from internships in college and was able to get on as a real estate development analyst, which was a fancy way of saying I ran a lot of spreadsheets.

I worked there for a few years developing mostly commercial office projects and multi-family, and then through that sort of real estate development path went to a smaller real estate development company and ultimately decided to start my own construction business in 2002.

Eric: *Describe for us what that start was like, and what did you do to get it off the ground?*

Charlie: It was an interesting time for us on a personal level. The stock market bubble had just burst. Along with the tech bubble in Seattle, the housing market was not that hot at the time. We'd just had our first child and I just felt like at that point in my career it was the right thing to do.

I knew I always wanted to start my own business and the timing was just right for me on a professional level. When I started, I had seen a lot of construction experience from the owner's side working in development for the previous four or five years, and knew what it felt like as an owner to work with a good contractor. And I thought that that perspective would be really beneficial to me in starting a construction business, as opposed to a lot of the other people that came up through a family of contractors or a trade and then decided to get into general contracting. Or, maybe someone who took more of a commercial route and went through the construction management school and then went to work for a big builder.

I came at it from a different perspective. I wasn't from a family of builders. I hadn't worked as tradesman. I didn't work in the construction industry beforehand. I wasn't at a big construction company, but I thought that my development experience would really lend a good perspective to construction projects even though we were doing much bigger stuff than when I started ACG.

That was my foundation or my building block of my business. From there, I just really strove to have a focus on professionalism. That was what we started off trying to deliver to our clients. We were doing much smaller projects at the time and were competing with people that didn't have the same educational background or professional background that I had had, and I thought that would be a good product to deliver to people that were looking at small remodels or small additions and could have the chance to work with someone who really had a professional background and have that flavor brought to their project.

Eric: *What were some of the things that you did proactively and intentionally to set yourself apart professionally? We all know there are stereotypes of the construction industry. There are a lot of opinions that the public has, some of them well-founded, some of them not. It's often not really hard for somebody to stand out in contracting if they'll just do some things to be different. Talk about some of the things you did specifically to stand out.*

Charlie: Sure. I think that some of this is the perspective I had at the time, and some is my perspective now looking back at the course of our business for seven years.

At the time, with the type of projects we were doing, we were competing against other builders who were mom and pop construction businesses, smaller businesses, where the owner of the company also did a lot of the field work and didn't really have an infrastructure to the business as far as personnel.

So I think a lot of times when you talk to people that have had projects that didn't leave the best impression upon them it wasn't necessarily coming from a construction quality or craftsmanship standpoint, it was coming from insufficient estimating, poor budgeting, poor planning or poor communication, or getting spread too thin where the builder would only show up every three days.

A lot of the feedback I have from my peers and just people who were hiring contractors, that was the repetitive story that you'd hear over and over again. When the project was all done, they'd maybe say "It turned out great, we love it. The guy did a great job, but it was a real bear getting to the finish line."

For us, I knew we could build well. I knew we could hire the right craftsmen and the right personnel, and I did a lot of the work myself in the field at the time. But I vowed that even if I was in the field eight hours a day I'd spend another five hours in my office at night doing estimates, doing budgeting, doing schedules and really making sure that when we were estimating projects and trying to solicit business that we didn't over-promise and under-deliver, and that our budgeting was accurate and that it was displayed in a format that was easy for the client to understand, but also provided a lot of detail.

A lot of feedback we had at the time was that clients would get a one-page letter that said "the project is going to cost *this*". So I developed an estimating spreadsheet that is real transparent to the client, easy for us to work off of and provided the right amount so it wasn't overkill, but with enough detail so the client could see what was going to happen, and how much things were going to cost.

Then as the project progressed we constantly would put the actuals against what we'd estimated so the client had this comfort level that things were going smoothly.

I'd really say it was estimating, scheduling, budgeting and then just the general level of professionalism. Whether that's communication, appearance, showing up when you say you're going to show up, just treating it like it was the most important thing for that client at the time and not just another small basement remodel.

Eric: *That's great. I think a lot of contractors reading this are thinking, "Man, that is awesome, but what Charlie created—the spreadsheets and all the detailed documents that he's providing to the client, I know my prospects* *and my clients would love to see those and I'd love to compete on that level, but I don't have a clue where to start creating those sorts of things."*

Charlie, some of your professional background helps, but was it a lot of late nights where you had to create stuff from scratch? Or did you have some tools or precedents that helped give you the foundation for creating them. If the latter, can you share anything that might give a contractor some hope that he could get to that level of professionalism?

Charlie: Yeah, sure. I'm going to answer that is two phases. The first part would be that I didn't really have a lot to start out with as far as template information. Like I said before, I didn't come from a traditional construction background, so I didn't have a bunch of budgets from a different company that I worked for that I could work off of to create our own budgets .

That wasn't how I came up. I didn't have a father or uncle in the business, so I didn't really start with something that was close and then tweaked it to make it our own.

It really did grow organically out of the needs of our business. So it obviously changed a lot over those seven years, but it also bears a lot of similarities with what we started with day one. I didn't really have a lot of template stuff to work off of and it was a lot of late nights and starting from scratch.

The second part is that I don't think it's as hard a people think. It seems daunting and I can see how a builder who's getting into the business and didn't have that background might say he didn't know how to do that. I would argue the opposite. The stuff that we have works great for our business and tells the story we want to tell when we're working with clients, it's also not exceptionally complicated. It's an excel spreadsheet.

All of our estimating we do now is still through excel, not a proprietary stock, or expensive software that you see at the builders shows. It's something that comes on every computer that comes with a home office package. It's not overly complicated to create so what I would say to people that are looking to do more of that stuff in their business and didn't think they had the tools, is that the MBA (Master Builders Association) offers courses in these programs.

Private schools offer excel classes or a Microsoft Project class, which handles scheduling. The level of that software versus the level we're using it at, we're just scratching the surface; we're doing pretty rudimentary things with that software. I would encourage your readers to look into that and not just assume that it's overly complicated or overly difficult to learn. If you can learn how to build a house, you can learn scheduling and estimating on Microsoft programs. It's not a killer.

The other thing I would say, is that I think it's almost paramount for success for your own internal purposes of estimating jobs and having budgets, where at the end of the day you make the money you think you're going to make on it.

It's just not practical to think, in today's day and age and with the level of competition that you can do this stuff on the back of an envelope or in a notepad and hope that when you build a million dollar house you make the money you hope to make at the end of the day. You need to have something internally to measure your own profitability and success.

With that knowledge and know how you can turn around and use that to tell the story to your clients.

Eric: *So Charlie, one of the things that I will note here is that of the folks interviewed for this book, you're one of the younger ones. A lot of the people* *that we're talking to have some gray hair, and some did grow up where their father was a contractor and his father was a contractor. Some have been doing it for decades.*

I think you bring a lot of value to this because you are relatively young and you've been in the business for seven years, but I think it will be inspiring to a lot of folks that will see that it's not out of reach like it seems, or they don't need to spend a lifetime at this to be successful. I'm grateful for that unique contribution you're bringing to this and I applaud you for what you've done. That said, in the seven years – let's call it seven-plus because you were involved in a different way before that – what are some of the lessons you've learned and what are some of the things that are golden nuggets for you as far as how you keep the ship on a straight path?

Charlie: Well, that's a good question and sort of what everyone wants to know. It's hard to boil that down to a handful of things, but I think some of the more important things that we've learned or that we set out from what we started is that success really breeds success.

Our main focus when we started was not about building the business. It was not about getting customers. It was not about profitability. It really wasn't about any of those things. My sole focus when we started was that the customer was happy at the end of the project. We would sacrifice profitability over that. We'd sacrifice working hours. We wanted happy customers because we knew that was the only way we'd get more customers.

My thought was that if we could get more customers that the business side of things would take care of itself. We would learn how to be better builders. We'd learn how to be more profitable builders. We'd be able to raise our rates over time as we established a relationship and established a reputation in the business.

If we got over concerned with profitability right out of the gate we were not looking long term enough. That was our main concern then and is still our main concern now. That being said, at some point your business has to turn a profit, but it was and is our number one goal in every project to have a happy customer; a customer that would use us again and refer us on to more people.

It's hard to get clients through other ways in the construction business. We tried mass marketing and some of those other things, but the old fashion word of mouth has been the best way for us. I think contractors need to make sure they focus on that, and focus on not getting hung up on whether their very first job goes well, or second job, or first year… it's about having happy customers and using that as your measuring stick. That's one of the main things I would say.

The other thing we tried to do – and you'll probably get other people that have a different approach – is we didn't want to get into the man power business. We don't self-perform a lot of work. We're strictly a management company.

We tried at times to staff up and do more steel work, do more framing, more finish carpentry, more concrete, things that are natural for general contractors. We found that it took our eye off of what we set out to do, which was to provide exceptional project management and exceptional professional oversight of a construction project. It started to split us into managing crews and keeping those guys busy and also trying to provide this management business.

We tried to stay more singular and our mission was to stick with providing what we wanted to do which was a top end, well managed, professional job site, communication, all the things we talked about earlier.

I think it's important that people realize what their strength is and that they stick to that and they understand not to get spread so thin that they can't deliver what they originally set out to deliver.

I think sometimes people, especially builders when they're first starting, see those other areas as profit centers and so they don't want to give that out to another framer or concrete guy because they have the know-how. But sometimes that doesn't work out long term for you. It splits up your business. Others have been successful at it, but it wasn't what we set out to do.

Eric: *Charlie, having gone that route of managing versus being more hands on with your own contractors or workers, does that make it easier or more difficult to maintain the standards of professionalism that you have set for your company?*

Charlie: Well, that's a really good question. There's two parts to that. The first part is the quality control issue which I think can be more difficult doing it the way we've decided to do it because you don't have as much control over the bodies on your job.

But I think as you grow and as you do more and more business and you're able to vet out more and more subcontractors and really establish a pool of subcontractors, then you can remove that element of risk from your jobsite.

I think early on for us that was an issue and though while we never turned over sub-quality work, we had to work harder to get the work that we wanted delivered to the client because of not having as much control over those subs. But, as we've grown and done more business with our pools of guys we've really mitigated that as a risk factor because they know how we build and they know they won't work for us again if they can't meet our standards.

So, we've been somewhat able to eliminate that risk. The thing that I would say is that if you go on vacation for a week or if your head guy gets hurt and is out for two weeks or you have a project that gets behind because of bad weather and you're having to divert a bunch of resources to catch up on that job and now you're light at another job, your work doesn't come to a standstill if you have a problem with your own personnel because we have more subs to pick from and more people to choose.

We're able to run multiple jobs and be more timely with those jobs. Whereas if we were more singularly focused on the labor side of things and if you get behind on a job it's tough to begin other work when you said you're going to start it.

So, from a quality standpoint, yes the quality control is an issue for a while, but from a time or speed standpoint, I'd say the opposite; we can build faster and be busy on a jobsite every day by using a subcontractor pool versus doing it all ourselves.

Eric: *Now before we move off the subject, there are going to be subcontractors reading this that aspire to be general contractors. There will also be a lot of folks that want to be subcontractors, or want to remain a sub. As a general contractor and one who hires subcontractors, talk briefly about how you find and choose subcontractors and also talk about, from the general contractor's perspective, what stands out about the best subcontractors you work with. What does a sub need to do if he wants to be the general contractor's "A" guy?*

Charlie: Well, finding the subs doesn't happen overnight and that's probably been one of our biggest challenges to deliver the kind of product we want to deliver and grow the business the way we want to grow it.

You can't just find someone you really like and then forget it. You still have to stay competitive. You still have to make sure your guys are delivering value, good price point, good workmanship. So even though we have the guys that we go to and are sort of our team, we're still constantly pricing them against other contractors or occasionally trying a different contractor that we've vetted out to our process that we feel comfortable with. You just can't get lazy.

As far as finding them, that process has been a real work in process for us and we feel like we're at our best point that we've been for the course of our business. We've found them through solicitation and other ways, but mostly from people I knew already getting into the business and finding a subcontractor that they like.

You find a good plumber that you like, and then you ask them, "Who are some good electricians that you've worked next to on jobsites? Who are some gas pipers that you've worked with that have been good?" Or, you find a framer that you like and they follow the concrete, so you ask the framer, "Who are some good concrete guys that you've come in after whose foundations have been square and plumb?"

And so, just sort of mining the other subcontractors for people that they've worked around jobsites with and delivered the kind of product they deliver because obviously they wouldn't be working on your jobsite if you didn't like them. That's probably been our best way. We get lots of solicitation. We probably answer 5% of them, so if I'm a subcontractor I don't know how effective that is for their time. In general, that's a tough way to break into our business.

It gets back to what we talked about earlier, which is word of mouth and making sure you walk off the jobsite and people are happy with you. It's tough to go to other generals and ask them who they use because once people get someone that they like they don't really want to be sending them all around town; they'll lose control over people they like having available for their projects.

It's probably not a lot different than how we built our customer base, which was just one client at a time, one customer at a time, making sure they're happy and satisfied. It think that in this business, specifically, people who deliver work where the client is satisfied and you deliver what you set out to deliver, on time, on budget, just do what you say you're going to do, the business growth seems to take care of itself.

I know that sounds really simple, but it seems to be the only way that I've been around in the business that works really effectively. We're constantly trying other ways, too, but just have less results with those methods.

Eric: *Meaning more traditional marketing methods?*

Charlie: Yes. We've tried mass mailers, we've done projects in a neighborhood and then sent out a flyer to that zip code with that project we just finished. It would make sense that everyone in that neighborhood would call you because if their neighbor built and liked you then why wouldn't they just save the trouble and go to you?

We don't have nearly as many hits off of that sort of stuff as we do simply from a client referring us to someone else, whether it be a homeowner, or architect, or structural engineer; that's 95% of the business that walks through our doors.

Eric: *That's a great segue. Every successful salesperson can often point to a lot of their success coming from good, strong referral relationships that they have. Not necessarily ones that they intentionally seek out and cultivate, but sometimes they are. I'm sure that's no different for you in your business. For a small contractor that wants to build their business and doesn't have some of those relationships in place, how would you suggest they go out and get those wheels in motion?*

Charlie: My advice would probably be how we did it because that's what I know the most. For contractors starting out, the builder community has this ant-architect mentality. They want to work with the homeowner. They don't want to be overseen by an architect, and that has been our gravy train.

It started off when we first started in the business. We had a couple people we knew that were the clients that hired an architect and hired us, independently of each other, and we got to know some of those architects and we became builders that those architects refer out to a lot when they get clients.

The architect is generally the first person that gets involved in a project, especially in residential. That starts with the architect before the contractor. An architect is charged with designing the project but then also making sure the project gets executed the right way. The last thing an architect wants to do is hitch their wagon to a builder that really makes it tough for them to deliver a project that meets their client's expectations.

For us, being able to deliver for the architects that we work for and making their jobs and life easier and making their client happy makes them want to do more and more projects with us.

Ultimately, it's up to the client to decide who the builder is that they want to work with, but as long as we're continuing to deliver value and we're competitive compared to our contemporaries then all else being equal, I think a lot of clients tend to go with a builder that their architect trusts and has used before.

That has been our single, biggest source of business, architectural referrals, with client referrals a close second. When you start in the business, you don't know a lot of architects.

Our plan, when we set forth, was really to target our circle of influence. People we knew from school, the neighborhood, soccer camp for our kids, and really get out the word that we were available to do construction for you.

So much of hiring the builder is the feeling of trust, and the feeling of a relationship, so if you already have someone you know who you're close to, that goes a long way towards getting you in the door with them.

That was our angle initially, to find 100 people that we felt we had a good relationship with and send them a letter, or call them, or drop by their house and tell them what we're doing. A grass roots approach, more so than cold calling or mass mailing to people we didn't have any sort of relationship with.

Eric: *Kind of a real world Facebook deal. You're asking people to be a "fan" of Anderson Construction Group.*

Charlie: Yes, that's very accurate. And then you get a couple of those people that need you to do a project for them, and they tell a couple people, and it just feeds upon itself. Now we do work for people where there are several degrees of separation between the client and the person that started the referral chain. It sort of "spider webs" out.

The commercial side has been a lot different for us than that. We are slowly making more of a concerted effort to break into the commercial business, but the playing field is completely different at that level than at the residential level.

Eric: *Great, that was going to be my next topic. You have quite a mix in your business of building custom homes and doing major remodels and then doing some commercial, and I'd like you to talk a little bit about how you've evolved to that mix. Is that the kind of mix you want to maintain, or is there a certain direction you want to go? Then, if you could close that loop by helping somebody who's reading here that doesn't really know if they should just go residential or go the commercial route, or both, and the pros and cons of both; and how someone might go about making that decision.*

Charlie: Well, there's a mouthful right there, but I'll do my best. When we set out from day one we wanted to have a mix of residential and commercial. That was a goal of ours.

The simplest way to say it is that if I could have a client trust me to build a two million dollar house for them, then why shouldn't that same client trust me to build their dental office or their tenant improvement for their law firm or their graphic design studio? That was my mind frame, which was, 'Why would you go through all that effort and foster that relationship and get someone to really trust you and really perform for them, and then not try to take advantage of all that person's needs?' That was the 'why' behind it and why I wanted to get into commercial.

I also thought it was a good diversification tool and if you could do both and not be totally reliant on the housing industry or not be totally reliant on the commercial industry but be able to go back and forth a little bit, I thought it was a good hedge against cyclical ups and downs of the construction world.

We're certainly not the only guys doing this, there's a handful of A+ builders that I could have subscribed to this same theory.

I would really caution your readers that they have to start with what they're good at, and with us it was the residential side of things.

There are a couple things we've done over the years that have been very beneficial for us. One of them was not growing too fast and not biting off more than we can chew because that gets back to my earlier statement of just not having happy customers.

Trying to get into the commercial world because the projects are bigger, or whatever your reasoning might be, if you don't have the know-how then it's a self-defeating purpose. There's no reason to do it because you're not going to do a good job.

For us, it's taken a while to get into the commercial business because we needed to acquire the know-how, we need to grow smart in that line of work. We needed to start with smaller jobs that we knew we could do and then slowly, over time, take on bigger jobs to get up to the level of being a legitimate option for people looking for commercial work.

So, if your readers are coming from a place of commercial property management and they know all about tenant improvements and re-tenanting office buildings, then maybe that's a good route for them to go, but if they're really coming from more of a residential background I would caution them to dip their toe in the water slowly on the commercial side of things because it's just not quite as intuitive.

You live in a house and you know how a house works. Commercial buildings just aren't the same way, they're built totally differently.

That is how we got into it. As far as the pros and cons of that and marketing to that audience, I think the main difference for us has been that level of professionalism that I talked about as far as how we wanted to run our jobs.

At the commercial level, that playing field is much more even. You're competing against people who are doing the same thing as you from a professional standpoint and from a tactical standpoint. It's not as much as a competitive edge at the commercial level as it is at the residential level, in my opinion.

It's really about opportunity, finding the jobs to get in on and getting a chance with the developer. Getting a chance with the building owner, because most of those people are already savvy. They're savvy real estate and construction people if they own businesses and operate commercial spaces.

They have a list of builders that they've used over the years and so breaking into that list of people that they call is tougher, and when you do break into it, just having a nice budget and a nice presentation and having a level of professionalism about you doesn't go as far as it does on the residential side. It's a slower market to break into. It's a little tougher to find the projects in the commercial business as opposed to the residential business.

Eric: *With the barriers to entry being higher, do you think that makes it a little more stable field to play in?*

Charlie: I don't know if I'd go that far to say that, because one of the things about the commercial property business, and this is why I wanted to maintain a residential and commercial side of our business, is that the projects tend to be bigger.

So it's a bigger volume job. Your margin is on a bigger denominator, so it can be a source of bigger profits, or more profits. Not necessarily the margin percentage, but more volume coming in your door. But, they're also fewer and farther between.

I know a couple of developers right now that are building commercial projects, and I know fifty people doing house projects. They're harder to find and there just are not as many of them.

So, I don't know if it's any more stable, because if you get all your eggs in that basket and then the two big projects finish up and you can't find something to fill that backlog with, you just don't have as many projects that you tend to work on.

And then, of course I'm speaking from where I'm at in the continuum. As you talk to some of your other builders who have been doing this for longer and they've been in the commercial business for twenty years, they might say just the complete opposite.

But for us, as far as breaking into that business (when I say breaking in, it's been an effort of ours over the last couple years) there aren't as many jobs. I would say that's one of the main things you need throughout the construction business.

I've talked to other business owners and other friends of mine that have businesses, and it gets back to having a level of client satisfaction. We might only have ten clients a year that walk in our door who don't know us that we do work for, even counting repeat clients.

Each one of those ten people represents a huge portion of our business and huge portion of what we do every day, so those ten people better be satisfied.

A restaurant might have 200 customers a day, so if one customer walks out with a bad opinion it's a small fraction of the customer base that you're playing to, so I think that's really unique about the construction business, especially a smaller builder like us who isn't multi-state and doesn't have a national presence. We have to treat every one of those clients like it's the end of our business if it doesn't go well. Finding that commercial client when we only have eight or ten clients a year, the commercial business seems to be more spotty than the residential business.

Eric: *That makes sense. Charlie, have you had any mentors that have helped you along in this journey of building your construction business and if so, let us know where you would put that on the scale of importance for somebody that builds their own business.*

Charlie: Well, I'm a big believer in the idea of mentors and mentorship. When I was in the commercial real estate business I certainly saw more of that and I was able to have more meetings with other developers, simply because they were willing to sit down and just talk to you about the business.

In the construction business, for me, it hasn't been as prevalent. We've certainly had people that have been advocates for us; clients that have been very satisfied that really helped build our business. They would really refer us and push us hard on people that were looking at a builder.

But, as far as a mentor that is in the construction business that has helped us develop our business plan and our model, the short answer is no. We've come across other builders and had small talks here and there or came to an event, or something like that. I might see someone every three or six months who I go to if I have a tricky job that I'm thinking about getting involved in and I want their opinion. We really haven't seen a lot of that.

It gets back to getting so guarded and so protective of your customer base. We may not be a threat to somebody else's business and we may be much smaller than them and not do similar projects, but you just never know what one job is going to turn into.

For us to do work for somebody and it may start out as a small job, that may be the lead to our next biggest job. I think people in the construction business and business owners in the construction industry might see you as bit of a threat. Not today, maybe, but a year from now or two years from now, and who knows what that one guy you help out could turn into for your business.

I wouldn't say I'd really be that way because it's having more relationships and knowing more people that always seems to help in business. It just seems to be the response I've gotten from other builders that I would have liked to have been mentors to me.

Eric: *It's interesting. It seems to be an industry where best practices and things like that are often kept close to the vest. Well, it sounds like you may be part of a movement to change that, which would be great.*

Listen, Charlie, why don't we wrap up here. Give us your final words for anybody that would really like to make a go of it in this business and really wants to be inspired, but also just be helped along to see that this really is a good business if you follow a few principles.

Charlie: Well, I would probably circle back to some things I've already touched on. I think you really have to take one customer at a time in this business. You can't look too far down the road and you can't get too focused on what's coming or what you want to build your business into.

You have to look who's in front of you right now and making sure you value and respect that client relationship and deliver what you say you're going to deliver.

I also think one thing your readers would be interested in is that it's not an overly complex business. It's not inherently heavy in technology. It's not inherently heavy in new age thinking. It's a pretty old fashioned business and I think sometimes people over complicate things and try to have a new spin on their business or do something too overt to set themselves apart.

I really think it boils down to simply doing what you say you're going to do. If that means the project takes six months then it takes six months. If it's going to cost a certain amount of money, it costs a certain amount of money. If you say you're going to give them a project update once a week, then you give it to them once a week.

But, you don't need to be overly concerned with new revolutionary takes on the construction business. People tend to be very satisfied and tend to go to bat for you if you can simply just deliver what you say you're going to deliver. That may not seem very novel, but it seems to be what is the truth and reality and we see it every day from our clients coming back to us.

The other thing I would say has been important for us, depending on what your goal for a business is and how much you want to grow your business and the size you want to be able to have your business, but for us a big turning point was getting a critical mass; getting to the point where we could invest in some office personnel, invest in office space and yard space and equipment, and being able to forego that money at the early stages of our business and reinvest it in the growth of our company and the personnel, because it's a hard business.

It's hard to be out there and be running jobsites and be running crews and then do all the business things that it takes to have a successful company.

If you can get to the point where you can have some division of tasks and you can have a real infrastructure where people in your business are charged with doing specific tasks, it makes your quality of life way better. It makes it so you can expand your business easier. It's easier to take on new work and new clients. It comes with the risk of adding overhead, but it gets back to where you want your business to be five years, ten years, twenty years down the road.

When we got to the point of being able to have that critical mass and have that infrastructure in place, it was just a big sigh of relief for us, personally and professionally, to be able to get to that point in our business. I'm glad we made the investment we did at the time to put that money back into the business and use that to grow.

These are just a few things that were keys to our success, and our happiness, too. It's a hard business. There are hard days out on the field and you need to be able to get to a point where you're not constantly running around like crazy trying to get your business to where you want it to be.

Eric: *Well, that's fantastic. Charlie, thank you so much. I'm looking at your beautiful website right now. If anyone would like to check out an abso-*

lutely gorgeous website for a construction company, go to www.andersoncg.com. Certainly, if you were someone looking to interview or look at a home builder, this would be a great place to go also. The work that he and his group have done is absolutely fantastic. I also want to bring up the fact that you're a winner of a pretty prestigious award here regionally for one of your big remodel jobs. Congratulations on that!

Charlie: Yes, thanks. That was a great job, a great team effort by everyone involved and we were super thrilled to be recognized for it.

Eric: *So, this brings me to two final questions, and you can be quick. How important would you say that a membership in Master Builders Association would be and also, as I look at your website, how important would you say it is to have a good website?*

Charlie: I would say the website issue has been a real strong point for us. I think we have a good website and I appreciate your comments on it. We spent a lot of time and a lot of thought getting it to where we wanted it to be and not just have it be a template style website, which you see from a lot of builders our size.

I wouldn't say it drives a ton of new business, but it really helps close potential business. I don't think people are out there Googling builders and finding a website and saying "This is a great website; I'm going to hire this builder."

There's much more of a level of intimacy involved when they make that decision. But, when you have someone that you're interviewing with or that you're meeting with for the first time, having a website that can tell a story, show a lot of pictures and where they can see current and past projects, without a doubt has been beneficial to the success of our business, as far as closing those potential deals.

The membership in the MBA, I think for a company that wants to grow and build the way we've built our business, it's essential. It just means you're committed to the building industry and it means you're in good standing and all those sorts of things.

As a small business owner, I haven't had as much of an opportunity to be as involved in MBA as I'd like. It takes being on committees and being on chairs. It takes a level of time that I haven't been able to siphon out of running my business to devote to that.

It's certainly something I aspire to, but right now we participate in a lot of their events and we try to just be a part of it to a degree that we can.

Eric: *Well, again, Charlie, thank you so much for taking the time here. I just know that it is going to be of great help to all the folks that are reading this. I wish you the best of luck and I know that you have an incredibly bright future ahead of you for Anderson Construction Group and all the folks involved.*

Charlie: Thank you, Eric. Any time I can help out I'd be happy to. Good luck to all of your readers out there and I wish nothing but the best for them.

Joseph Irons
President and General Manager
Irons Brothers Construction

About Joseph

W e now have the privilege of talking with Joseph Irons. Joseph is the President and General Manager of Irons Brothers Construction, based in Shoreline, Washington. His hands-on experience and commitment to the homebuilding industry began at a young age and has helped him structure his business into an award-winning design/build remodeling company. He is committed to continuing education and has achieved the highest designation of Graduate Master Builder (GMB) from the National Association of Home Builders University of Housing.

Joseph has also achieved the designations of Certified Graduate Remodeler (CGR), Certified Aging in Place Specialist (CAPS), and Certified Green Professional (CGP).

He has served as an executive board member of the Master Builders Association, of King and Snohomish Counties, and currently serves on Seattle Central Community College's Wood Construction Center Technical Advisory Board. He is active in the Remodeler's Council, The National Kitchen and Bath Association (NKBA), The Rental Housing Association's (RHA) Associates Council and the Greater Seattle Business Association (GSBA). He is a National and State Director for the NAHB and the Building Industry Association of Washington (BIAW) and is actively involved in committee work.

Joseph plays an active role in the communities where he lives and works, and is a member of Shoreline's Community Emergency Response Team (CERT) in addition to volunteering his personal and company's time to many local charities and organizations.

When not working, Joseph enjoys traveling, snowboarding, motorcycling, running, biking, and spending time with his family and friends. He is the proud father of an amazing little girl and thinks the best part of every work day is making his clients' remodeling dreams come true.

Eric: *You sound like a very busy guy, Joseph. Thank you so much for joining us today.*

Joseph: Thanks for having me.

Eric: *Why don't we start out by having you tell us about your background and how you got started in construction and take us though the highs and lows of your career and bring us up to the present? It sounds like you have a lot on your plate and we'd love to hear about how you built your business.*

Joseph: I got started helping my father and older brother remodeling ever since I was little, a toddler almost, swinging a hammer. I've always enjoyed it, had fun doing it, but never thought it would be my career. I was in high school still swinging hammers, making money on the side.

I've done lots of other jobs as well. In high school I worked at a large national grocery chain. Part of that experience helped me look at the organizational structure, customer service aspects, retail sales, learning a "customer is always right attitude". I also worked in produce stands in high school which helped me realize that quality in appearance is what really sells stuff, along with communication and service. It's not just the cost. It taught me that you have to have high value, high standards to have that customer or client return and want to do business with you consistently.

I did some telemarketing after that as well. It was an owner referral program, which again went back to customer service and the quality of the product we were selling, to making sure people were happy. A lot of that helped me in the business aspects of building a company versus actually the hands on technical. What made my company today is actually attending a lot of the educational seminars and conferences, and not just in the construction industry—although I attend several of those each year. But in general business because a lot of the local chambers of commerce, the local business associations, etc. have great networking opportunities such as luncheons where you can meet good advisors.

Another key element of my business is knowing the right people—attorney, insurance broker, CPA, etc. To make sure that in everything we are doing we are getting the best benefits. For instance if we're going to buy a new vehicle I'm going to run it by our accountant first to make sure we know the best way to purchase the vehicle that will give our company the best return. If I'm going to take on a new product line, like a commercial project or a larger residential project than we typically would do, I'm going to talk to our attorney to find out what I need to draft in the agreement to protect our liability and protect our client's assets, as well as check with our insurance broker to see if we need to adjust anything within our policies to make sure we are fully covered. And again, that's not just to protect us, but also protect our clients. If we're not looking out for our clients, we're not going to receive referrals from those clients on future jobs.

Most of our clients we complete multiple projects for. When we're done with their projects, and in the middle of them, they're referring us to their friends to do their projects.

I think that's sort of it in a nutshell, a little background, if that helps.

Eric: *Yes, definitely. Now, talk a little bit about the kind of business that you guys do. You've got a number of different designations. Talk about what kind of volume you do, and the business mix.*

Joseph: The type of services we offer are broken into three divisions: residential, commercial and small projects. Current volume is just under a million. We've been growing 10-30% every year for the past ten years. When we started out I was barely making a salary for myself. Now we have seven staff currently. I'm one, and my wife is the office manager.

Types of projects… On the residential side we do bathrooms, kitchens, additions, whole homes. We do a lot of specialty work in the homes as well. A lot of tile, stone, finish details.

That's one of the things I love about our business; being able to design and customize our products to our clients.

We do a lot of Aging in Place work, that's one of my certified designations. We use universal design to make sure that door openings are wider so people can walk through, etc. We call it "aging in place", but it's really "better design."

For example we have grab bars in our office showroom bathroom that people are amazed by; you don't even realize they're there. So grab bars are not an upsell to our clients, but a necessity they need that doesn't look like a commercial bathroom. Stepless grade changes, lever handles, décor light switches are some other universal/aging-in-place standards. Along with aging in place also goes child safety. Anything we're going to build we want to make sure it's safe for all ages. I have an 18-month-old daughter so it definitely hits home for me.

On the commercial side, we do small tenant improvements, multi-family, non-profits, churches, retail spaces. Commercial is a different monster. It is about 30% of what we do, and we also do small projects as well. So the three service lines are residential, commercial and small projects.

Small projects are anything from hanging a door or window to decks, railings, a laundry room conversion, etc., things that you would typically consider handyman work. But if our clients want that work, we want to be their first call for all their home's needs. If we're not the right company, we're going to get the right person for them.

Eric: *Now, do you use subcontractors? And if so, what percentage would you say you subcontract versus using in-house employees?*

Joseph: It depends on what we're doing, Obviously, all our electrical and plumbing is subcontracted out. A lot of our concrete forming. A lot of the rough specialty trades we subcontract, but it also depends on the size of the project. If it's a small kitchen remodel or addition we may insulate in-house, or we may subcontract it out. If it's a small bathroom we're probably going to drywall it ourselves. If it's a kitchen or large addition we're generally going to subcontract the drywall out.

We always look at it this way: is it more cost effective for our staff to do it, or for a subcontractor to do it? And our subcontractors are specialists in their area and typically more cost effective to complete that portion of work. But the smaller the project the more cost effective it is to do all work in-house. And by cost-effective I mean within budget for the client. If it's something that we need a specialist in and we don't have someone in-house that can do it, then we are definitely going to subcontract it out.

Proportion-wise, maybe 40% of the work we do is subcontracted. We always look at cost, but we also need to look at schedule. If our guys can do it and it's going to cost another $100, we're going to have our guys do it if it ends up being a week earlier. Schedule is huge for our clients. We want to make sure first of all it's done by the date they expect it to be done, which we establish at the beginning of the project.

Eric: *So, I'm glad we get to cover an area that hasn't come up in any other interview, and that's Aging in Place work. I think it's interesting, because that segment of the business is poised to grow quite a bit as the baby boomer generation ages.*

So, I'm guessing maybe that had something to do with getting your Aging in Place designation. I'm curious to know, how much do you focus on that portion of the business, and is that something you're looking to grow? And lastly, is this something you'd recommend to someone getting started in construction, or looking to grow their business? Is that an avenue you suggest, or something you'd recommend they add to their mix?

Joseph: I would definitely recommend anyone to add it to their mix. Most Aging in Place work is just good design, like I said earlier. When someone is designing a space, they should be designing it for someone who is not only aging in place, but suppose your client might get in a car accident and be injured for a few months. If they have three steps at their entry, it's going to be a lot harder for them to use their home. If they have a multi-level house it's going to be hard for them to go up and down the stairs.

If they do live in a rambler, keeping everything with stepless grade changes and no transitions is always ideal. We take out a ton of bathtubs and install showers. There are lots of people who find it so difficult to lift their legs over the bathtub every day; they would choose not to bathe as often.

So do I recommend this work to other contractors? Yes, I highly recommend getting training in Universal Design and Aging in Place. According to AARP (American Association of Retired Persons) the baby boomer is the largest growing population out there.

With our personal projects, we design it into a project, because I think it's the right thing to do. For example, if we are redoing a client's entry, we'll suggest removing the step if possible. There are other benefits, it's not just for those using a walker or a wheelchair. If they want to wheel a barbecue around the house, or a garbage can, or a cooler, it's much easier. It's easier living overall if we can get rid of the steps.

Eric: *Yes, I think that's great. I think the message here for the reader is that you really ought to consider ways that you can add that to your business arsenal. One other question I would ask about that is what would you recommend for marketing? What have you found to be effective ways to generate business in that segment? Are there certain folks that are good to network with, are there certain areas that you advertise? How do you market for that?*

Joseph: We market a lot back into the community. We give back to several charities; we do a lot of walks for causes. One big thing we do is building ramps for an annual event with the Master Builders Association. They have a Care Foundation that builds ramps for needy people that can't afford to build a ramp but definitely have a need for one. Most of them are wheelchair bound and can't get in and out of their homes.

I'll go ahead and get the resources and labor needs covered, we go out and in one day build a ramp. The ramps I choose are typically twenty to fifty feet and probably $5,000 to $10,000 ramps, and these are built at no cost.

So we give back to the community that way, and then send out a press release about it to get a little promotion from that. That's just a stepping stone.

A lot of colleagues of mine network with occupational therapists. The biggest thing I think for marketing I've seen is to document your work. Not enough people document with before and after photos. Show people that your work is going to look nice and be eye pleasing.

The problem is a lot of contractors get the short end of the stick. A lot of homeowners hire their brother-in-law to do work and unfortunately he didn't know the proper building codes, building techniques, or use the proper building materials. They use indoor materials outside and it rots out. They use inadequate materials that are not meant for the install so it doesn't hold up. They don't frame properly, so it won't support the weight of someone in a mechanical wheelchair that's a few hundred pounds.

So I believe the best thing to do is document what you do, and when you talk to people let them know, 'Hey, we can make this for you, let me show you some examples.' It doesn't always have to be a big ad in the newspaper, you just need to get the word out there that there are good options for people.

Eric: *That's good. You hit on something there. We've interviewed some long-time veterans of the industry, and something everyone has hit on is that when they look back and identify some of the keys to their success in the business they always talk about community involvement. Rotary, chamber of commerce, serving on different committees, charities, etc.*

It's kind of just how life works, isn't it? When you give in different ways, you often get back all that you need. You certainly can't go into these situations and join these groups and things like that and walk in with your hands outstretched like an empty cup and say 'Could you fill this up for me?' You can't do that, you can't have that mindset. But if you go in with a good attitude and a giving heart, a lot of times it's going to come back to you and maybe even more so. It sounds like that's probably been a big key to your success, has it not?

Joseph: It's been a huge key to my success. It's one of our core values. We have some pretty basic core values. The first is high quality craftsmanship. Superior customer service is also one. Community involvement, green practices, professionalism, education and safety. Those are the key values at my company. Like I said, community involvement is one of them. I get the labor needs, and it's not hard to get our staff to want to help. Actually, most of the time when we build those ramps I was talking about, I past employees from years ago who come back just to help with those events.

We have a staff of seven, and typically we have twenty volunteers at the events helping build the ramp and most of those are current and past employees, and some friends of the company or subcontractors we've asked to help, and they're always more than willing to help. With the community work, just the team building alone on those days is amazing. We're giving back to someone who needs it!

A lot of clients have the resources readily available to build a ramp, get an elevator, get what they need. But the ones that don't have the resources, sometimes their needs are almost ten times, because they've been living without it trapped in their house. It's a health and safety issue. So when we go out and build them a ramp, we're just sort of floored, you can really see their appreciation.

Community involvement and being involved with the chamber and giving back is important. I co-chaired the Rampathon committee several years as well. I've seen it from the point of taking applications in, to asking big suppliers to help donate, and little suppliers too, anyone who can help. Also talking to other builders in the industry as well, asking for help in building the ramps. We get the resources, but we need people to actually help with the building. Last year we built over 30 ramps. My company can't build 30 ramps in one day at no cost. But I know enough people I can ask to step up and help make it happen.

Eric: *That's wonderful. Good for you, that's fantastic that you guys do that.*

So, let's switch gears a little bit. You have been in and around the construction business for many years now; you mentioned swinging that little hammer as a toddler even. As a professional in the industry, talk about some of the qualities and practices that you have observed in the successful contractors out there. We're all very much aware of the things that unsuccessful contractors do; they're the stereotypes which we've all either heard or experienced: "He doesn't show up on time. He didn't finish and never came back."

So many people have those nightmare stories, but it doesn't have to be that way. What are some of the things that you've observed over the years in successful contractors? But also, you're one of them — so what are some of the disciplines, if you will, that you have implemented in your business to ensure that your company will be a success?

Joseph: Some of the successful things we've implemented… One of the core values we mentioned is education. I wouldn't be successful without giving myself good education, that's from industry involvement; I have lots of certifications. Most of the good contractors I know have given themselves lots of professional development personally.

Going to local trade shows at a minimum. But going to regional and national ones and actually learning from other people in the industry. A lot of things I think that unsuccessful contractors have, besides not providing themselves some development of their profession, is poor communication. I can go on a project to do a bathroom remodel, and if I don't tell the client that they're not going to have that bathroom for the duration of the project and they're expecting to be able to use that toilet every day, they're not going to be happy from the beginning.

Before we do every project, no matter how small, we're going to have a pre-construction conference with the client outlining things like the schedule, what entrance to use, what materials will be used, where to store materials, where to set up the saws, setting up protective products as well. If we're going to come in and we're only working one room, we're going to put down carpet masking in the walkway to get to that space.

I think the biggest thing, getting back to your question as far as successful versus unsuccessful, is giving the clients clear communication and setting it up so everyone is on the same page from the beginning.

I have a pretty thick construction agreement which outlines what we are going to do, as well as what our clients are going to do and can expect.

Back to the pre-construction conference. One of the things on there is to remove any art work from the walls. We don't want to be banging on the walls and next thing you know the client's painting falls off – no one is going to be happy. We are the experts in the field and if we don't educate the clients, we are just going to have a bad name.

Another thing I think that a lot of people experience is the horror story of hiring their brother-in-law or their cousin, or a friend of a friend, and they're not a licensed, bonded, registered contractor. We're one of the only trades out there where people consider us the same as a brother-in-law at times.

I always recommend that contractors follow local building codes and regulations, but also being registered and licensed in the cities they work in. Also, staying in your scope of work. If you're a deck builder, and all you know how to do is build decks, then you probably shouldn't be bidding on a second story addition without help from a professional who knows what they're doing. You're going to go out there and not do a good job, most likely, because you don't have the expertise to do it. You need to say no to the wrong client.

When I started out I definitely didn't make a lot of money on my first projects. They were things I was interested in learning and knew I was not going to make the money on the project because I'm learning to do some of these aspects as I go. I would say I was fairly well educated, I had the right staff, the right systems in place to take on the project, but there's no way with my experience level at the time on some of the projects that I was going to be the most cost effective on it if I were to charge my full rate for the work.

So I guess some projects I should have said no to because I didn't make money, but others I considered it a marketing expense, or a training expense.

Hopefully that covers enough. The biggest thing, I think, is clear communication.

Eric: *I think that's great. You brought up something that I think is just fantastic. I hope some of the readers will put this into practice. I bet if you interviewed a hundred people who have had construction projects done on their home, I bet you wouldn't find three to five of them whose contractor had a pre-construction conference with them. Maybe there's some informal chit-chat, but it conveys such professionalism when you sit down with the client and talk about things that will affect them and their project. You mentioned some things that I bet most people would never even think of.*

Joseph: With our pre-construction conference, most of the things are from past experiences. Where do we park the vehicles so we're not blocking the neighbors, or someone's spot? Are there any restrictions on parking? What are the garbage days? If there's an alley, we don't want to be back there unloading stuff and there's a garbage truck honking at us. Where's the service location, as far as the water, electrical, so we're not bothering our client in the middle of the day and wasting time?

Most of these are things that make us more proficient at our job, which saves our clients money. So anything that isn't black and white we try to clarify ahead of time. A lot of this is in the agreement. With the pre-construction conference it's site specific. If we're working for a client with two homes, or two different projects in the same home, it's specific to where we're working.

It also includes their emergency contacts. Do they have pets? Do they have children? Do they have house cleaners, dog walker, nanny? Who should we expect to come over? We clarify who has access to their house and we also use a lock box for access on site.

But as far as successful, unsuccessful, clear communication is important and I prefer written because we do have lots of subcontractors and staff. We have site notebooks, so if our staff is not on site there is still communication to find out what is planned and agreed to for scope of work.

Not all of our sites have full spec details. Some of our plans are sketched on paper which is just as good. We just want to make sure it is sketched out so everyone's on the same page. They want a blue ceiling; we need to make sure it doesn't get painted pink. The more that is in writing, the better, because we can make mistakes.

The more that's written down, there's less room for misunderstanding. It takes a few more moments up front, but it builds our relationship with the client and leads to more future business with them and their friends.

Eric: *So Joseph, one of the things I have seen consistently in a lot of the successful business folks that I have talked to is that in addition to running the successful business and learning how to do that, there has also been a focus on themselves; developing as a person, to be able to do the things that it takes to run a successful business and grow it and lead it. Talk a little about that if you would, about ways you develop yourself personally and keep yourself sharp.*

Joseph: Personal development is important for many reasons. I always have considered myself a lifelong learner; I'm always going to learn from my mistakes. Personally, I think if you don't learn from your mistakes you can't expect different results from what you've been getting.

I said prior that I attend several industry trade shows, conferences, motivational speakers, you name it. If there's an event and it sounds interesting, I'm at it. Some people ask how you find time to do your work. Well, if I don't do it, I'm not going to grow myself or my company, so I plan it into my calendar.

Some other things that have helped me to grow are being able to delegate; hiring qualified people to do the job. There are several hats in the business, but in my opinion the three big ones are sales and marketing, administrative, and production. It's hard for me to run all three myself, and administrative is my least favorite, so that why I got an administrator and office manager. Taking those baby steps and one of those hats off helped my company to grow. Now all the invoicing and paperwork, people in my office complete that. Yes, I oversee it, and I create the systems and they jump through those hoops, but I'm not the one doing it day by day. I also have to do my part and fill out the paperwork when I'm on the other side. I wouldn't ask someone to do something I'm not willing to do myself.

Another big hat is sales and marketing. I enjoy the sales, but I want to be able to say no to the wrong clients. So personally I do the majority of the sales and marketing in our company. Other staff do help out, and everyone on my team definitely does sales either in the field or in the office. They can sell our company everywhere but in the end I want to be the one that's meeting clients and doing the site visits and the proposals.

In my line of work, production is building stuff in the field. I enjoy that, I started out doing all that, but as the company grew it could not continue growing if I was just going to wear that hat all the time; I couldn't lead the company in the direction I wanted to. So I sort of stepped back and became the General Manager and let someone else take over production. That was one of the hardest things to do.

First of all you have to find the right people to do those jobs and still oversee the work. I'm selling the jobs, I have to make sure what I sold, my staff are completing.

With delegating I guess the biggest thing is being able to step back and ask people to do it, and not micromanage so much. Being organized is another one, even though my wife would say I'm not the most organized, I try to be as organized as possible. To help get organized I have my staff document to keep organized on site logs, vehicle logs and such.

With professional development, I don't feel it's just important for me, but I also feel it's important for my staff. If I don't train my staff, I can't expect them to grow.

Personally I think my staff are my face. When they're walking into a store and have a uniform on or are talking to our clients, they are on stage representing me and my company. Products change, manufacturers change, even building methods change. What was okay to do ten years ago, sometimes is the worst thing to do today. So we want to make sure they're learning what's current.

As far as professional development, there are a lot of different aspects. But those are some of the things that have helped me grow the company to where it is today.

Eric: *Thank you for sharing all that. I think that will be a big help to our readers.*

Well, in wrapping up, one thing I think everybody would love to hear from you, having been around the block a couple of times now, is what advice would you give to somebody just starting out or maybe in the early stages their business and they'd really like to grow it or take it to the next level. Maybe talk about it from the standpoint of if you were starting over right now, what would you do and how would you go out and build your business as solidly, effectively and quickly as possible.

Joseph: First of all, I wouldn't say quickly is the best way to start a business. You're going to have to step back and first of all see what you want out of the business. I started mine relatively quickly, but I also had to fire some of my best friends and family because they weren't the right people in my business.

So I would take it slow. If you're doing it yourself that's great, if you're getting partners in, make sure they're the right partners and have clear expectations as to who is going to do what. So when the business grows you can actually have a succession plan for the company, and not just end it and be unhappy.

Also find good advisors. I've gone through different attorneys, insurance agents, CPA's, bookkeepers, because at first I was growing too fast. If I'm hiring a CPA I want to make sure I'm getting the best benefit, my company's getting the best benefit, and we're able to pull reports for review and growth.

Make sure you have an attorney who is familiar with the kind of business you're in. Make sure you have an attorney that knows construction law; one that knows in a certain situation the verbiage needed to be printed to protect you as well as your client or subcontractor, whatever the case may be.

Also be sure to have a good pool of designers, architects, engineers. They're going to be not just a referral source, but support to build your projects.

Also suppliers. There's the big box stores out there, but they're like our 7-11, we don't want to go there unless it's an emergency. We go to our local lumber yards. We support local community businesses. This is because the local stores generally have better knowledge, better building products and more access to suppliers.

I've had too many instances where our clients go into a big box store and their employee tells them the wrong advice. I can think of one recently where the client went in and asked for insulation; they told the employee the joist size and what the contractor recommended, and the store employee said no, you don't need it that thick. Unfortunately our client put it in, trying to save money and then we had to tell them unfortunately the building inspector won't allow that because it doesn't meet current code. So after that the client asked us to remove it and reinstall the right stuff. So essentially they incurred the cost of removal, reinstallation, and the cost of the insulation. Almost double versus if they went to a local lumber yard where they probably would have been told to buy the right product and best practice.

Nonetheless, I would say think about it, write a good business plan and marketing plan. Those are things I didn't start out with and I wish I did. It would have saved me a lot of money, a lot of time, a lot of headache. Hire good staff, with good experience but great attitudes. I've hired great staff who were great at the trade but didn't have the best attitude. It wasn't a good fit and I had to let them go later.

Make sure you have a written contract on your projects; agreements with your clients to make sure that everything is clear and the communication is clear up front. It's a lot easier to write it up front than to try to rewrite it after something has gone wrong.

Make sure you have a good team of subcontractors. A lot of work you're not going to be able to do, especially if you don't have that much expertise in it. So make sure you have good resources. That can be as simple as joining a building association, talking to your peers, seeing people at meetings and learning more about them. For us, we don't typically let a subcontractor go on site until I've either seen their shop, showroom, or a project; pretty much a thorough interview. We have a thick subcontractor agreement as well, to make sure they're going to follow through on what they said they were going to do.

Also learn to say no to the wrong client, that's another big thing. Don't get stuck into the job that isn't going to make you money, only headaches.

Get involved in your local chamber of commerce, your local building association and your local business association. I'm not saying get involved by just signing up and becoming a member. If you sign up and become a member, go to meetings and talk to people. Let them know what you do, let them know how you can help them. See how they can help you.

That would be my little nutshell as far as if I was going to start over again.

Eric: *Well that's perfect. I think that's going to be of great help to a lot of folks. Hopefully they will benefit from the insight of guys like you who have been around the block, who have done different things that worked and didn't work. Basically you're a virtual mentor.*

What does a mentor do? He helps you navigate waters that you haven't been in before that he is familiar with. That's what we're doing here. We're trying to draw on some of the successes and failures that guys like you have experienced and help folks that haven't gone in those waters yet. I think I can probably speak for most folks that will be reading this that your advice and insight and experience is very much appreciated. So, thanks a ton for taking this time, Joseph, I really appreciate it.

Joseph: Thanks for having me. Hopefully people learn from this and don't make some of the same mistakes I did and actually do things the right way, because it saves a lot of time and headaches, and in the end, obviously the dollar.

Eric: *Yes, without a doubt. Well, it sounds like you are definitely on your way. I wish you the best of luck with your business.*

Joseph: Sounds great, thanks Eric.

Brad Decker, President
Decker Development & Construction

About Brad

B rad is the President of Decker Development and Construction. Decker Development builds and owns high quality retail strip centers located adjacent to or near major malls. Brad has been doing that since 2002 and prior to that spent about 20 years building mainly residential homes and apartment buildings and holding those.

He later sold off most of those properties and got into commercial, and saw a lot of success in both realms.

He has an incredible story and has a lot of wonderful things to share and I think you'll very much enjoy this. Brad is a wonderful guy, has two great kids and a beautiful wife, and just has an enviable life in many ways. He's just such a great and humble guy and does wonderful things in his community, in business and in his church. But it hasn't all been easy, as Brad will share with us, so we're very lucky to have him here today. Thanks Brad!

Brad: Thanks, I hope I can live up to that.

Eric: *And them some, I'm sure. Why don't you start us off by giving us your background? Tell your story about how you got into real estate and take us through some of the twists and turns of that career and bring us all the way into the present.*

Brad: Well, I'll start with college. I went to the University of

Washington and in a fraternity met a good friend of mine, Walt Towns, and we started a business together. After a year working together, I was excited about the business, but realized it didn't really have much potential.

We ended up selling it to another friend and we were looking for a new business and we went to one of those "nothing down" seminars. I remember purchasing a Wright Thurston teaching about how to buy apartment buildings, and the power of real estate, learning that about 90% of the wealth of the world is held in real estate.

We said, "We should do this." We had no money, so nothing down purchasing was really good for us because that's all we had, so it was just our time.

We partnered up with another friend, Craig Dawson, and we went and started to do what the tapes told us to do, so we went out and we started purchasing homes and apartment buildings with nothing down.

I distinctly remember once buying these 23 units with only six bathrooms and trying to figure out how to get the money to fix it up; with nothing down there wasn't much of a cash flow.

We were struggling. We had one friend who was working so we would split his salary and then Walt, after he graduated, started working and would split his salary. The three of us would work at night and I would work during the day after my classes, and realized that we weren't getting a cash flow. We had to fix them up and sell them.

By doing this we were able to create a cash flow, so we changed our focus to buying homes and apartments, fixing them up and selling them. So this was in the mid 80's after the high interest rates and things started to take off, so we partnered up with another gentleman who builds apartments and we asked him how he did that and started working with him building apartments.

He would take 50% and we would take 50% and so that's how we started to get into building homes and then building apartment buildings.

His plan was to build and sell so we did that through the late 80's, and then in 1990 I remember very specifically that we had 1,000 units that were out there in contracts. We hadn't closed on them but we had invested in the earnest money plans and permits and through '90 and '91 started to get these ready to build and there was no financing, similar to now. There was liquidity crisis in the S&L debacle and there was just no money out there.

The interesting thing is they changed the rules. The requirements, the down payments to build, increased to 30% to purchase the land. Also, you had to put up 30% of the capital for the construction.

Now all of a sudden we had been playing by one set of rules and by the new set of rules we had 1,000 units of apartments that didn't make sense to build.

We had to spend about five years to work through that and with that process learned a lot about dealing with money, taking risk, figuring out what's acceptable risk or not for my lifestyle and realized that it's better to earn small amounts of money and do it a lot of times, rather than try to make a lot of money in one or two locations.

So, after prayer God kind of got us through with another plan. But in the meantime, I had to figure out something else to do, so started to do Riches in Renovations because we had been doing that for the last seven years and had a good plan doing it.

We started doing seminars called Riches in Renovations and had people hire me as a consultant. I did this for about four years to provide the cash flow to get us through the lean years of the early 90's until I could actually build out the product that I had, because I had to do that for free.

Eric: *In these seminars you were basically teaching people to do what you guys had done before. So you were taking some of the knowledge and experience you had, sharing it for pay via seminars, and these folks would hire you to hold their hand and help them do what you had done.*

Brad: Exactly. So during the day I would be building the products (the homes) and at night I'd be doing the seminars or working with the clients to help them renovate the buildings or homes, to be able to turn them around for profit or to evaluate whether to purchase them or not purchase them. So it was a good value for them and it provided the necessary income for us to pay for food and shelter at that time.

Eric: *I got you off track a little bit and want to get you back on, but that strategy of fixing and flipping, especially earlier in this decade, became incredibly popular. You go to the bookstore now and you can find 100 books on how to fix and flip properties, so it's become very crowded and diluted. But the way you did it and what you taught folks, is that still a good route to go for somebody wanting to build a business or career in real estate?*

Brad: It can be. What we're looking for is several twists, so if you just buy a house and fix it up and sell it it's a hard way of creating a living. Sometimes you do well and sometimes you don't and it depends on the market, too. As you know, markets go up and down and what we don't anticipate is when the market goes down.

If you average out over a long period of time you do okay, but you're just doing okay. We look for a chance to buy a house that you can fix up that might have an extra lot on it or you could add to it, so you could add another unit to it in townhome style and then subdivide them off.

We found our profits were maybe $10,000, and if we did well they were $50,000, but didn't cover the hindsight when the market turned down. Then we would lose ten, twenty, thirty thousand.

Also, when you buy and sell, you have to pay ordinary income tax. So you have to take that into consideration when you're doing that plan and set aside sufficient reserves to get you through the lean times when the market does go down or when the market just gets cold for a while and it doesn't sell for six months and you have to wait and feed the property.

Looking at that, you can do well, but you can do better if you look at trying to make wealth little bit by little bit. What I mean by that, is that the plan the Lord had given me was finding a way to help people, and He gave me a plan to help mainly single women with kids build three- or four-bedroom homes and provide shelter for them at affordable costs.

So what we did is build hundreds of three- or four-bedroom homes throughout the Seattle area. So we basically focused on one plan, one area and just stayed consistent and persistent on building those and making sure they met the plan.

By doing that, I was able to know my costs very well, know what I could pay for the land and know what I could get for rent. You also learn that you're not always going to receive your rent;

you calculate what you average over a long period of time on your rents, or net income.

That we did for about 12 years. We could only pay $15,000 per unit and didn't want critical areas, so these need to be relatively flat, of which there are not a lot in the city of Seattle. At that time, being able to pay that price when other people were paying over $100,000 for a lot was very difficult.

We were able to do it through creative ways of purchasing, a lot of estate sales, pre-foreclosures. Being able to find the land was a gift from Heaven, or manna from Heaven, as we call it, but needed to find at least four sites a year where we could do four to six units on each site. Some we did up to 24 homes.

We did that through 2000 and focused on that and it was very difficult because you saw other people building the townhomes and doing really well in the late 2000's.

In 2001, when we had the terrorist attack, rent dropped at that time, so that was a hard time where we had the rent drop almost a 1/3 in some locations. We focused on one plan, but I recognized that that season would end. So we tried different things, like office and mixed use, to see how those worked and at that time didn't like either of those plans. We were just trying different twists of the same plan to see if we could make it achieve our end goal better.

We had a specific plan on what we were trying to achieve each month, both on the cash flow, the cost to build it or the equity and keeping our loan to values low in the 50-60% so that we weren't over leveraging, but with very tight budgets.

The other lesson was focusing on the pennies and the dollars so that we could achieve the goals that we had laid out. In 2002, I felt God telling me that it was time to sell all of these, so we started selling all the homes and apartments in 2002 and switching over to commercial.

So, buying commercial buildings or commercial land to renovate or build retail strip centers (high quality strip centers) next to major malls was our goal. Across the street was what we were shooting for, or within a block.

So, in 2002 we started selling off everything and by 2007 had sold all but two homes when the market had changed. I remember August of 2007 I had to reduce the price by $25,000 on these last two homes and just didn't want to do it because I felt the market would come back. Little did I know it would drop even further and might not come back for another five years. That's just a short version of my story.

Eric: *Thank you, Brad. Talk about some of the differences. What has this experience been like on the commercial side and how would you compare that to the residential side? What are some of the things you like and dislike about both?*

Brad: I thought the transition would be relatively easy from building homes and five story apartments with post tension slabs and two levels of underground parking, to building commercial centers. It was actually very difficult.

You have to be much more detailed with commercial because every square foot has to be accounted for when you're laying out a site. You have to maximize everything in order to make them work because we had a very hot market at the time. There's a lot of competition to purchase these centers and find a way to make them cash flow, to make our profit margins, to keep our debt ratio low. You have to be much more detailed when you make the commercial centers.

The risk is a lot higher, too. When you have homes, you have a lot more people willing to step in. When somebody moves out, you go in and fix it up and rent it out to a new tenant and you have a lot more people willing to pay the rent.

In commercial, you have higher swings of rent and you have fewer people willing to lease those out, even in great locations. That can be difficult and can cause people without sufficient reserve to not be able to make it. So I think learning to have higher reserves in commercial, being more patient, I think you have a higher risk and probably higher reward. You have a little more complicated tenants in businesses. Those are the more difficult things.

The positive is, the tenants care about the property. They want to make sure you have a high class, high quality location and building and want to see it maintained and taken care of and are willing to pay for that. With the triple net, that's part of the cost. The tenants do pick up to pay for that, so you can have the funds to take care of that.

The other positive is that it's much less management intensive. They are a lot easier to manage once you get good tenants in them. Unlike residential, we'll have a constant turnover just of life. In commercial you usually have less turnover.

Eric: *That learning curve you talked about with commercial, how did you navigate that? Was it trial and error? Did you have people you worked with that helped you learn that side of the business, or have mentors?*

Brad: You know, I don't think I would have done it unless I went into partnership with somebody who was an expert at it. I went into partnership with a gentleman who was a money lender to us back in the late 80's and who was one of the people who we had to work for years to pay back.

But I think because we were willing to do that, he was willing to work and go in to partnership with me in the retail seminars. That's what he specializes in. He's an incredible salesman. His strengths compliment my strengths. My strengths are more on the construction end and his strengths are on the sales end.

He had been doing retail leasing for most of his life at Coldwell Banker and knew the market extremely well, so going into it would have been very difficult to do by myself. Having a partner or mentor who knows the industry allowed me to be able to enter that commercial market.

Eric: *Let's talk a little bit about the construction side of things. Over the years, on both the residential and commercial side, you have had a lot of experience with contractors. We've talked to contractors who never do anything but subcontract. We've talked to some who do a lot of the work with their own employees and do a lot of the building themselves. Talk about how you have done that both on the residential and commercial side, and then talk about your experience working with and observing both successful and not so great contractors over the years.*

Brad: Okay. Well, we have relationships with contractors that go back 20 years that we still work with. We have ones that we work with one time and then we'll never work with again. I think the difference between the two is the difference between somebody who cares about you and is willing to help you achieve what you want and the contractor that only cares about themselves and achieving what they want.

The subcontractors that we have consistently worked with have been fair and have had steady pricing. Even with the contractors that we've worked with for 20 years, we still bid them out occasionally and make sure they're competitive. I think they're consistent in their pricing, they're consistent in customer service and they're willing to take care of us, and when they can't they just simply let us know in a fashion that just explains it: 'It's not that you're a less of a priority, I just have to take care of this commitment before I take care of your commitment.'

I think the number one thing for us is their heart, knowing that they care about us. Number two, their pricing, that they're consistent. I don't know if that means they have a consistent margin, I just know that our pricing on our end is very consistent for what we're getting. Although it does go up, when I compare them to other people they are fair.

Eric: *If you had to pick out the three qualities of a successful contractor that you've observed consistently over the years, outside of what you described as what makes for a great relationship for you with the contractor, what would you say those would be?*

Brad: In my niche, of the qualities that I've found, it is the care of the owner about my needs. My scheduling and my pricing and getting the job done right. It's not a verbal, it's a *non*-verbal heart issue, that if somebody really cares about you, you can tell, even if it's over the phone, or if it's in a proposal, you know it.

Also, the crew that comes out and does the job, that they have good quality people that do the job right and if they make a mistake, they come back and fix it without any issues. They don't complain, they just do it.

Lastly, they don't take on too much. They're available to meet your needs in a reasonable period of time.

Eric: *It's interesting—I've heard a couple other folks mention that, including an architect we've spoken with. That's something he looks for as well: contractors that don't try to take everything that comes their way, but are responsible about it. If you take on too much you're probably not going to do any of it too well and that doesn't make for a lasting business, typically.*

Brad: The other thing that I've been impressed with is that some contractors do anything, which is not right. The good contractors focus on certain things.

When I made the switch from residential to commercial, very few of our subs could follow us because they were very good at residential and then when I tried to bring them in to commercial most of them were just not able to do that. They shouldn't because it's not what their specialty is, it's not what they or their guys are really good at.

I think the ones that do well have a very specific niche, even if it's residential, it might be low-end, mid-end, apartments, or high-end, it's important that they stick with that niche and they do it really well.

For commercial, it's hard for a framer to do both, to frame wood and metal, they're just different. A contractor should pick a very specific niche and focus on it, and then just try other things on a limited basis to see if there's an opportunity to make a twist and make it better.

The subcontractors we work with that specialize in what we're trying to do are focusing on the right niche of general contractor or developer.

Eric: *That's great, thanks Brad. So, let's transition toward the latter part of our interview. One of the many reasons that I wanted to have you be part of this is because you've been very successful in real estate development and have a pretty unique background professionally, having seen success in both the residential and commercial areas.*

What I also admire about you, is that in your personal story you've experienced some incredible highs and lows and continued to persevere. I read a lot of books and I love reading biographies about successful people, and one of the things you learn about almost all successful people out there is that they persevered through sometimes seemingly impossible and insurmountable circumstances.

So, I'd love to have you talk about some of the highs and lows you've experienced and some of the things that have helped you as you look back, to get through those tough times and to make yourself even better, because I know that there are a number of things that you would attribute to that and I think your story and some of the things that you can share would be an inspiration to a lot of people.

Brad: Well, it was hard when we had lost everything and were in debt to other people and had to work five years to pay everybody back. That time was like a fog; you can't see anything except the step ahead of you. We survived by having faith and trusting that God has a plan for me, and just taking that step with persistent and consistent action.

Some other people switch and try different things, but, as we've talked about, when you start something new it's like a 747 jet sitting on a tarmac. You have to give it all your energy and it still doesn't move. Then it starts to slowly move and it takes all this energy and fuel to get off the runway and then you've got to put in another ten years to get that up to cruising altitude, as far as time and energy.

So when you're working and you've learned something, if you switch fields, it's like being in that airplane on the starting ground again. So, I thank God that I didn't switch.

I stayed doing the same thing because I had learned something from the past. I had learned something from my failures. I don't know if they were my failures, or if they were just natural things that happened in the world. The economy drops.

Look at today. A lot of people will not do well because of the economy. Did they fail? No, they just had natural consequences and that happened. So learning from that and modifying it so you don't make the same mistakes, and get going again. Take that consistent and persistent action, knowing where you want to go and knowing where you need to go and focus on that. You don't focus on other things during that time.

I had to let a lot of other things go. I focused on church, family, work and working out, and that was all I could do during those lean years, giving a good five years to working out of debt.

Eric: *I'm kind of hearing from that explanation that goal setting is probably a discipline of yours. Is that correct?*

Brad: It has been. It isn't as much now, but it has been a very crucial part in the past. If you're in a plane and you're flying to Hawaii, if you don't know where you're going, it doesn't matter which way you go. You've got to know where you're going so your subconscious can be that onboard computer and can help you when the winds of life push you to the south and to the north and you can redirect and keep heading to where your goal is.

If you don't have a goal then you don't have a direction. You need to have a direction, especially in business, of what it is you're specifically shooting for. With written goals that you can measure along the way, you can make sure you're getting what you're trying to head for.

Eric: *Can you point to any books that you can say were really instrumental in your development as a person and businessman over the years?*

Brad: Yeah, I have a library full of them. But I think the lesson that I learned from all of them is to invest in yourself. So, back when Walt, Craig and I started in college, we started buying tapes. We started buying books and I still continue on that habit, 25 years later, learning from the best.

You need to learn about finances. You need to learn about your personality to keep you moving. You have to learn about your industry. You have to learn about family, being a good husband and father. I would say it's the habit of persistent education.

You're never done, and I still have a long way to go. So, it's not one book that did it, or one tape, but it's reading books to learn. It's listening to tapes or CD's in the car to grow, and consistently doing that.

Eric: *Good stuff. So Brad, to wrap up, for somebody who's reading this who is maybe just starting out or within the first year or two of becoming a contractor, or even somebody more established but wanting to grow. If you could give them a few bullets of advice, what would they be?*

Brad: Start with the end in mind. Know where you're going. If you want to be a subcontractor, what size do you want? What lifestyle? What income do you need? Work with the end in mind and work backwards to achieve it.

Also, understanding your talents and working within your talents. Know what you're good at. Ask your friends, have testing done to know where your strengths and weaknesses are. And where your weaknesses are, if they are bookkeeping for example, then make it a learned habit for bookkeeping and detail work.

I think the most important thing for businesses is really knowing where you're making money and where you're losing money. If you don't know where you're doing well or not doing well, and why, most importantly, then you'll continue making mistakes. That would be the second thing.

Learn the things that you need to know the basics, selling your product, taking care of your clients and knowing where the money flows are. Do those three things, and if you're weak in any of those then make them learned habits where you can have people teach you how to do them well.

Eric: *Great advice! Brad, thank you so much for taking the time to talk with us today. I think it's going to be very valuable advice for the folks that are reading this. Thank you again and best of luck with whatever chapter is next for you.*

Brad: You're welcome and I wish you God's speed on building Bridge to Profit. I think it will be great tool for people to use to help them grow personally, to be part of that education that everybody consistently needs.

Eric: *Thank you very much. You take care, Brad.*

Howard Chermak
Founder and President
Chermak Construction

About Howard

Next up in our series of Champion interviews is Howard Chermak, President of Chermak Construction. Howard started Chermak Construction back in 1974. Chermak Construction grew out of Howard's need to generate income to finance his college education while attending Western Washington State University and later as a means to supplement his teaching income while working for the state of Minnesota as a speech therapist in their school system.

After working several summers as a carpenter while in college and later as a teacher, Howard found that not only was he enjoying the building process but he was also finding success and satisfaction in it.

In 1974, Howard made the decision to move back to Edmonds and enter the construction business on a full-time basis. He started with a local builder architect as a master carpenter involved in all phases of residential and light commercial construction and he was soon in full charge of the projects he was working on and made the decision to start his own business.

In 1980, he founded TRF Construction as a remodeling and construction company. In 1989, Howard incorporated and renamed the company Chermak Construction Inc. That year he also received his Certified Graduate Remodeler designation. The designation is awarded by the National Assoc. of Homebuilders Remodelers Council to remodelers who have successfully completed a prescribed course of study as well as demonstrating that they have successfully operated a remodeling business. Howard was one of the first builders in WA state to receive this designation.

Since its inception, the company has been involved in all phases of residential light commercial remodeling and it's truly a full service remodeling company. They do consistently $5-10 million a year in revenues and have about 35-40 employees.

They'll do a custom home every year or two and do some low-rise commercial work, but both of those things only comprise about 10% of their business. It's mostly residential remodel work; that's really where they specialize.

In addition to a whole slew of awards for their work, they've also been consistently a nominee or winner of awards with regard to being a great place to work, of which Howard is very proud. Howard is a family man and loves working in the business. Again, we're so lucky to be talking with him today and drawing on his many years of success in this business.

Eric: *Howard, welcome and thank you!*

Howard: Yes, thank you!

Eric: *So, start by telling us about your background. Tell us about preconstruction and how you led into it and then give us the highlights and lowlights, if you'd like, of your career and bring us up to the present.*

Howard: Okay. When I was in high school, a brother-in-law was helping put himself through law school at the University of Washington by remodeling in the summer times and on vacations for family members. So I went to work for him and basically was the "runner" from the basement floor of a home up to the top floor. I was a material taker on the way up and a demolition person on the way down.

That was really my very first job in construction and I rather enjoyed some of the work I was able to do. Some sanding and finishing and some painting as I began to learn more about the business. The same person's father also owned an aluminum window factory and I went to work for him in summer times, also, right after high school and during college.

I was able to use a lot of different kinds of equipment, tape measures, saws, welders and things in that aluminum window factory. At the time I didn't realize it, but I may have been the only non-union worker in the place. I found out a bit about unions and how they work and why it was necessary to belong to one at that time.

After I graduated from college I went to Vietnam for about a year and a half, came back from that and worked in construction to sort of "find myself." I applied for jobs in teaching. In college I graduated with two degrees, one in speech therapy and audiology and one in elementary education.

I was looking for a job after I came back from Vietnam. However, levies were not passing at that particular time and very few special education teachers were being hired, which would have been my areas of expertise.

I heard about a job from my parents who happened to be living in Northern Minnesota, where I was born, and I drove back there to interview for the job, more or less on a whim, and actually got the job.

I stayed there for two years and in the summer times I would turn to construction in order to earn money and found that I really did enjoy the carpentry and the creation of things.

After two years of teaching I realized it was not feeding me, it wasn't my passion. So, I returned back to Seattle in 1974 and, again, turned to carpentry and remodeling projects in order to feed the family.

I hooked up with an architect who also fancied himself as a builder and he would choose very difficult lots to build on because he felt that he could design a home that would adequately fit the lot and other contractors would have trouble doing that. Then we'd build on those particular lots.

Over the six year period, we built about 45 houses, some of them custom, many of them spec houses. In 1980, the interest rates went to 20% or so and it effectively shut down the business that I was working in with the architect.

I again turned to remodeling and started my own company, working for friends, and branched out a little more and a little more. The first seven or eight years through the 80's I pretty much worked by myself, maybe with one crew that worked with me.

As we reached 1987 or so, I hired the first person in the office and that was the start of expanding the business. As you go through the remodeling business, you begin to realize that you have three main areas to concentrate on, sales, production and administration.

Production is the first I gave up because I realized I could sell and administrate more than I could produce as a carpenter. Over the time, I have given up more and more of both the administration and sales to other people, but those are the two areas that I still concentrate in as we have gained employees and as we have grown the business.

In 1988, my current wife came to work for me, we were not married at the time. We were definitely under a half a million dollars a year when she arrived and as we grew the company together, in 1997 we realized we were best friends and we got married. We continue to work, to this day, in the company together. We enjoy the sense of community that the business gives us and we're having the time of our lives, quite frankly!

Eric: *That's wonderful! So, despite what the economy is doing at present, the business is still thriving. What do you attribute that to?*

Howard: Well, a couple of things. The first one is a vision from the year before. In doing the business plan it was not going to be as easy to sell and we likely were going to have to take a look at the first decrease in business in a number of years.

We planned that it would be more difficult to sell. We planned for less volume, if you will, and secondarily, we started a plan for what we might do as a company in order to help ourselves if we were going to have less volume. Then what were we going to do in order to make ourselves successful? Where could we look that we had not been looking that would help us weather this downturn?

Eric: *Can you go into some detail of what that plan looked like? What are some of the things you started to do specifically that were maybe different from before, assuming that before the downturn, with your company being fairly mature, you weren't having to do a lot of marketing anymore? At this point,* *your business is probably mainly referral based. From a marketing stand-point, what did your business look like prior to the downturn and what were some of the things you started to do differently after?*

Howard: It is interesting. We do a lot of home shows in con-vention centers and things around Seattle and we also do home tours through our local Master Builder Association. Those are the main ways, other than community involvement, which is another big marketing piece for us; the joining of rotary clubs, chamber of commerce, the Edmonds Community College Foundation, the Stevens Hospital Foundation, etc.

We've been involved in all kinds of community based organi-zations over the years and at the current time, of course. We de-cided we would even go after that more.

At Chermak, we have an all office meeting we call the Vision Team. About every month and a half we meet and we discuss matters that are pertinent to the company and try to get everyone in the office, about 14 or 15 people, involved in "How do you think we're doing?" and "What do you think we ought to be do-ing?".

In this vision team we came up with a concept last year that we needed to concentrate on marketing, and about how to mar-ket our business in a new way because we felt we needed to reach out in order to survive, in order to keep any kind of volume in the business going.

Each individual was asked at each meeting what they thought was their best marketing avenue and what they thought would be a good avenue for the company.

That was the beginning of the vision team meeting and it be-came a marketing meeting, quite frankly. Each month, as we would meet, we would talk about what had worked and what had not worked and what we thought might work.

That's how we changed the marketing. One of the really solid concepts that came out of this that we had not mined our past clients very well as a marketing prospect.

We started to do different marketing pieces to our past clients and that really generated quite a bit of what it is we're doing. So out of the longevity that you speak of certainly we have a good history of clients and that really helped us a lot.

Eric: *I'm glad you brought that up, and thank you for sharing those things, Howard. What a great revelation for you guys, and I think so many business owners really take for granted their past customers and I don't necessarily mean that in a negative way. But I think business owners often make the assumption that their client was happy with the product they produced or the service they rendered and so 'Of course they're going to think of me when they need something else done', or 'Of course they're going to think of me when someone they're in contact with mentions the need for a project to get done.'*

As we all know, we get busy and are just bombarded on a daily basis with so many marketing and advertising messages from this world we live in, that to make that assumption, that past customers are, of course, going to think of you, is really missing the boat for a lot of folks.

As I'm sure you found by proactively going back and cultivating those relationships and, as you said, mining those contacts, I think there's so much hidden business that could be cultivated by a proactive effort there, which is so much easier to do and so much less costly than going out and getting new customers.

Howard: Absolutely. The cost is minimal and they already do know your work. It's interesting that it wouldn't come up before this, that we really needed to proactively go after our past customers and simply ask them if there was anything that they were thinking of.

That simple question really brought a flood of work into the company and it continues to do so because we now have a system of touching them periodically without becoming a pest. That would be one of the concerns in touching old customers also.

Eric: *So, do you do that by sending a newsletter or something like that? How do you stay in touch?*

Howard: We haven't done a newsletter. We have a sales trainer that offers a free newsletter and we've decided that doesn't really work for our clients. That's something that if we were to touch them once a quarter with a newsletter, I'm not sure that's our best way with our particular clients.

We do it with a personalized piece that either announces something or we might display a project that we're particularly proud of in a little letter and just ask them how they're doing and find out if there's anything we can do for them. We're trying to do that about three times a year.

Eric: *Okay. What do you suggest for somebody who's reading this that just had that light bulb moment and realized, 'Gosh, I've really done a poor job staying in touch with past clients to leverage my database and generate new business.'*

What would you recommend for that first contact? Would it be a letter that is maybe somewhat personalized just saying, 'Hi, haven't been in touch for a while and wanted to check in.'? What would be the best way to initiate that new, regular contact?

Howard: Do something seasonal. You could write a little note for those that you were very close to, or simply sign your name and touch base in order to break the ice.

In other words, if there were a special occasion that you knew of, one of the most effective ways that I have read of is that remembering important dates in their lives and sending either a birthday card or some kind of personal contact if you possibly could is a wonderful way of staying close.

That likely does not work for someone who is just thinking about how to re-contact people, so I would send a more personal letter to the contact and see if there's a response out of that.

Eric: *Okay, great. I want to circle back to something else you mentioned with regard to community involvement. You know, rotary and chamber of commerce and things like that, typically those things take time to develop. You don't just show up for your first rotary meeting and walk away with a referral, unless you're real lucky. Often those types of involvements are more effective if you don't go in with a mindset of what you're going to get out of it.*

For someone who is early in their career as a contractor or maybe is a little more developed but really hasn't been involved too much, would you say that would be a pretty effective way to start laying a bit of a marketing foundation by looking for some various things in their community that they can be involved in?

Howard: I absolutely do. The one thing that believe I have learned from the community involvement is that the rotary clubs meet once a week, and I find that to be a very effective way to meet and get to know people. If you join a committee or if you join in with someone in rotary on a particular project, you will meet not only once a week, but also more often outside of it likely.

Again, more connection to people, more people to connect with. Yet chambers of commerce, if you meet generally once a month, I find that hard to get any kind of consistency. In other words, if you miss a meeting, you're two months in between your meetings and that's a hard way to keep any kind of continuity.

If I were looking for the very first meeting that I were going to go to, I would choose something like a rotary club or Kiwanis, or that type of organization that meets once a week, in order to make more connection.

Eric: *Okay, good. I've had the privilege in talking to a number of successful contractors, successful business people, for this book and invariably what I find is that successful people are often able to look back and point to a few disciplines that they were consistent about in their personal and business life that they can really say helped them to be successful as a person, as a business owner.*

If you had to pick a few things that, in looking back and probably right up to today, are things that you do, what would those things be? Can you talk about that a little bit?

Howard: Yes. I think that the confidence level that came for me back in 1979. I was considering whether I could stay employed in that business with the builder architect, simply because he didn't have a lot of work at that time.

One of the things I felt to be very, very important was that I control a job from the very conceptual part of it to the completion where I handed over the key to the owner.

For a friend, I found a designer to design his home on a piece of vacation property near Seattle, and worked with him through the design and then actually went up and built the home by hand myself.

What I'm saying is that at some level in the remodeling construction, there are so many facets that you need to know and so many little variables in there that unless you are a niche remodeler, such as a kitchen and bath person, or a siding and roofing person, there are so many areas that you need to know that there is something you need to do that will give you the confidence that you know everything there is to know about what it is you're building.

In that sense, I think that's where I started in 1979 and I realized that I could do it from the ground up. I really didn't build a new house for another ten years, but what I knew was all the parts and pieces that needed to be put together in order to do the house and how they fit together. I think that really helps if you're going to be a full service remodeler.

If you're not a full service remodeler and you're a niche remodeler, I would say you would just simply find out everything there is to know about the kind of project that you're going to be doing, kitchen or baths, for example.

It seemed in my business, that one of the most difficult things to do often times is to sell something. It's much easier to work on a computer. It's much easier to work with employees. It's very easy to do the accounting. However, one of the most difficult things to do is to sell a project at a profit.

I knew that whenever my company was at a base point, I need to sell something. That may be the focus that saves the company. It's much easier to work on a future business plan or almost anything, except selling, and yet if you're not selling something in our business, the engine doesn't start.

Eric: *You know, that's interesting you brought that up. One of my first bosses, early on in my career after college, taught me two things that I will carry with me forever. One of them was "Run when you have to, walk when you can." He said to just always remember that. Sometimes you have to run, and when you need to, run hard. When you can rest, go ahead and rest, so you're able to run hard again when you need to.*

The other thing he said was, "Get in the habit of asking yourself, on a regular basis, 'Is what I'm doing right now making money?'" We know that sometimes you've got to do stuff that you can't really tag a dollar value to, necessarily, but for the most part your time is extremely valuable and you really have to be as productive as you can be, especially when you have employees.

You've got folks depending on you, and they have families depending on you. So that habit of asking yourself, "Is what I'm doing producing revenue and profit for the business? Is what I'm doing something that someone else could be doing so I can be doing the things that are utilizing my strengths and helping produce revenue effectively for the business?"

Howard, if you had to start over in the business, talk a little bit about what you would do. The reason for asking this is that there are a lot of people reading this that are very early on in their career, or haven't developed their business much, and maybe feel a bit overwhelmed that they don't have a lot of clients under their belt and don't have a lot of referrals coming in.

It's a tough economy right now, but there's still business to be had out there and if somebody wants to be successful and put their mind to it, they will. If you were in their shoes, starting from scratch right now and going to build it based on what you've learned, what would your first three to six months look like?

Howard: That's a good question. I think I would start with keeping my vision fairly wide for what residential remodeling means. I think one of the successes of my business over the years has been that I've kept it full service.

I have competitors who at times have said, if it's not a $50,000 project, then we won't be doing it. Those were obviously in good markets and things, but I have always felt that the more kinds of projects that I can include, the more possibility for work for the company. I have purposely kept us a full service remodel company for really two reasons.

The first one is that I love the variety and I have had more people tell me, that work with me, that they love the variety and they simply could not stand to build widgets all day. The variety comes up as one of the things.

The other thing is it allows you to keep busy when others may not be able to. I like the broad approach if you're starting your new business and the idea that you'll take on just about anything that you can.

Eric: *It's probably quite difficult for you, having built a business as large and successful as yours, to imagine starting over.*

Howard: When a person starts in this business, it's not as the business manager; it's generally as the carpenter. I'm not certain how many companies start from that position, but, of course, since mine did, all of them must have!

But, I wonder if the entrepreneurs have begun a business by having business and then hiring carpenters and things. That's an end that I did not come from. So that's a tough one for me to see. I think that if you were a carpenter based person that is growing a business, then I suspect that is quite different than a person who may have carpentry skills but wants to hire people in order to do so, a little like project managers. That's a little different business than what we're talking about.

Eric: *Now, that brings up one question that I forgot to ask you earlier. What percentage of your work is done by subcontractors, and whatever that percentage is, how did you come to the decision to structure it that way?*

Howard: That's a great question on subcontractors. Originally, very little of the work in 1980 and probably through 1983, was done by subcontractors. As the business has grown I have used subcontractors and I'd say that around 20% subcontractor would be through the year 2003. About 20% would be subcontractor and probably in that same time period as much as 30% would be my own labor on staff.

Starting in about 2003-04, the market started to grow and carpenters were less available so I began to use more subcontractors and now, with our labor in house becoming more efficient, certainly in the last few years, we have switched the percentages where now we are 35% subcontractor and maybe 20% in house labor. Some of that is because carpenters were not available in 2005, 2006 and 2007. This year, we are trying to feed our carpenters more work and so we're bringing those subcontractor percentages down. We're back in the high 20's with them and we're up into the low 20's with our own labor because we're trying to keep our own people busy and yet stay effective monetarily.

Eric: *That's really helpful, thank you. Howard, if you could crystallize for the folks reading here in a few sentences just some words of encouragement or advice, some nuggets of wisdom that you could give to them to help in this journey, what would they be?*

Howard: The *people* in your business are the most important. I think that my wife, Judy, that works in the business with me, has brought the caring to construction. I believe that when a construction company cares, it becomes something very special.

I think that you can do beautiful work and do lots of things, but when you build the sense of community within your company and with your customer base it's great, and obviously with the people in your community itself. When you build that sense of community, that sense of belonging, I think you build something very special.

I have struggled over the years with whether we are a family, as a small company, or whether we are a team. I've always struggled with the word "divisions" within a company. I don't like those terms, but I very much would say that the sense of caring for one another and that connectedness and the sense of a community of people working together and a common goal is the highest, I believe, that we can achieve.

Eric: *Wonderful. Expand on that just a touch, if you wouldn't mind; I think that is so important and so powerful. What do you intentionally and proactively do to help cultivate that?*

Howard: I think it is caring about each individual in the company and understanding what it is that they are having to deal with; understanding what they can offer up; asking them what it is they might like to be doing; asking them what it is they think I might be doing. In other words, an openness in communication that allows for people to say, 'Well gee Howard, I know you're the president of the company, but I think that if you do "this" it would be better.'

We have a little bit of an issue with field workers and office workers in remodeling construction, and yet to try to bring the fields into the company and making certain that they're not alienated, making certain that they have a voice, I think would be the most important thing that I could suggest to anyone, making certain that there are not power camps of the office and power camps in the field. 'Those people in office don't understand.' I think that togetherness, with everyone moving in the same direction, the company can far exceed your expectations.

Eric: *Yes, that's powerful. Well Howard, thank you so much. Just from listening to you speak about your company and how you've built it, I'm not surprised at all that it's very successful. I think what you've shared is going to be of great value to those reading and they'll be very inspired and motivated to build something like you have. Again, thank you so much for taking the time to be part of this.*

Howard: You're welcome, thank you!

Eric: *Take care!*

TOOLBOX

Notes from the Champions

- Always adhere to the basics:
    - Be professional.
    - Show up on time.
    - Finish the job.
    - Communicate.
    - Don't take on more than you're capable of.
    - Make happy customers and get referrals.
- Get involved in builder associations, business groups, community groups and charitable causes.
- Leverage your database. People that know you, especially those you've done work for, will be the first to refer you or use you again – if you stay in touch!
- Keep the Caring in Construction.
- Continually improve and educate yourself. Read books, attend seminars, listen to cd's in the car. *__See page 229!__*
- Pursue certified designations. Not only will it give you credibility, it will allow you to pursue new and additional revenue streams for your business.
- Use clear, concise, professional and detailed contracts, estimates, budget forms and proposals.

PART THREE | "Bring in the Specialists"

Unique Perspectives

Have you ever noticed that you sometimes get the best feedback and advice, whether it is related to work, relationships, sports or whatever, from an objective "other party" who doesn't know much about you personally and is therefore able to simply observe your performance?

I guess the question answers itself as evidenced by the number of consultants there are these days. But do not miss the fact that the value of a consultant, or objective observer, is not just in the fact that they can watch and listen and analyze without their opinions and advice being influenced by prior knowledge of personalities, events, historical performance, etc.

They also come without the baggage associated with your (or your organization's) ingrained habits, paradigms, excuses, and other things that keep you from seeing your situation from a higher, more objective level.

For this reason, I decided to bring in some specialists who aren't themselves contractors, but have many years of firsthand experience with contractors, and really their livelihood depends on them.

Please do not jump to the conclusion that the only valuable interviews in this book are with the contractors. I think you will be pleasantly surprised by just how powerful, pertinent and of considerable importance the specialists' viewpoints and comments are to your business.

So, read on, and take notes. The Specialists' suggestions and ideas about *your* business, if taken and applied, could help take your business to the next level and beyond.

Mike Dunn
President
Dunn Lumber Corporation

About Mike

Mike Dunn is the president of Dunn Lumber Co. in Seattle, WA. Dunn Lumber was founded in 1907 by Mike's great-grandfather. The company has approximately 300 employees, does upwards of $100 Million per year in revenue and has a dozen locations.

It is an impressive company that has seen great success. Over the years Dunn Lumber has grown from a small family-run company to a modern corporation really adhering to best practices based on expressed values. Dunn has not only expanded its business plan, but also focused its efforts, and the owners and employees are very excited about where the company is going in the next decade.

Mike is a family man with three children; two daughters and a son, between the ages of 15 and 21. He likes to invest time in relationships, whether it's at work, home or in the church. He's of the belief that all significant work happens in the safety of trusting relationships and he works hard to provide those secure places.

His great-grandfather brought the company to Seattle in 1911 and it has been there ever since. Mike started working for Dunn Lumber as a boy, worked there all through high school and college, and after college made it his career.

We're very lucky to have him as part of this book and get to hear about his experience and his perspective on the industry from the viewpoint of a lumber retailer, as he's been involved in many ways over the years. So, we're going to do our best to glean as many nuggets of wisdom as we can from his brain and his experience.

One additional thing to note is that he is a voracious reader. It seems like every successful person I talk to has an insatiable appetite for reading, and especially of what one might call success literature; books on leadership and entrepreneurship, and biographies of men and women who pursued success and excellence in their lives and work.

Eric: *Mike, we're so lucky to have you here, thank you so much for joining us.*

Mike: Thank you, my pleasure.

Eric: *Well, I'd love to have you just talk about your background and tell us about what it was like growing up in this wonderful family owned lumber company and give us a description of growing up around that. Then launch us into your career within it.*

Mike: Well, I was fortunate not to live under a lot of pressure about taking over the business and the job was an opportunity to make some money.

It was pretty fun work. I got started part-time in junior high school at about 13 and when college came around nobody offered to pay for my education, so it just made sense to stay here. Back then, I could make enough money in the summer to pay for going to the UW and live in a fraternity.

When I fell in love with economics in college, the business started to take on more interest and about that time my dad told me that if I was interested in the business he'd like to have some kind of a commitment. He said we'd go a different direction depending on my interest.

I said I was ready to commit and we ended up opening up a yard in the Totem Lake area in Kirkland, WA and it was opened just shortly after I graduated. I moved there as a manager, I'd been working at the sales counter all through high school and college.

That was an immediate success. That was late 1978 and 1979 and was a huge year in the lumber business and we were busier than crazy. We were only open 8-5 Monday-Friday and 8-noon on Saturday and we all worked all of the hours.

We didn't get out of there until 2:00 or so on Saturdays. We'd usually sleep all Saturday afternoon and just barely be ready to come back to work on Monday.

It's been a good ride. I spent about 25 years doing the purchasing for Dunn Lumber and that was a lot of fun. New relationships and the lumber people, in general, are great people. I'm very fortunate to be part of such a wonderful industry.

Eric: *So, what are some of the major ways you've seen the industry change over the years? Have there been certain times or events, certainly changes in the economy, like the one we're experiencing right now, that bring about* *change? Talk about some of the ways it's changed over the years and how Dunn has had to change as a business.*

Mike: Well, probably the most major impact in our industry ever was the advent of the box stores. In the early 90's, when the box stores started opening up in Seattle, we lost eight major competitors. We saw sales slide for a couple of years and it was very tense.

Most of our competitors tried to accommodate by becoming box store-like and that never works. They just didn't have the ability to compete at that level. We determined early on that we weren't going to change and we changed very little.

We expanded our hours a bit, we ended up going to Sunday openings, but in general, we didn't change our product mix. What we found was, we did best by competing on quality and service and as we did that we tended to attract more and more of the remodeling contractors which made up for a lot of the DIY (Do It Yourself) business that we were losing.

I was just kind of getting my feet on the ground in terms of the buying during that time and what I was finding was that it was a lot more fun to buy the quality materials that made our contractors happy, and that even though they said price was really important to them, they would pay a little more to get the better quality.

Over time, we upgraded many of our lines until we weren't such a direct comparison to the box stores. Our quality of lumber was better, our plywood was better, we were carrying encapsulated insulation versus the open batts.

A lot of different product lines gave us a niche and we rode that niche and continued to improve on it. Now, as the box stores are disappointing more and more people, we're finding the Do-It-Yourselfers are coming back.

Meanwhile, we're trying to be the all-in-one provider for our builders and customers by purchasing more of a stick frame lumber provider that can provide the competitive lumber packages as well as getting into cabinets and specializing at some locations in doors and windows. The opening of the box stores was the boost that got us going into being more proactive about the niche that we're in.

Eric: *It's seems that your task was really to ensure that your customers didn't see it as an apples-to-apples comparison, that you guys are oranges. It wasn't a choice between you guys and Home Depot because there is no comparison. I'm guessing that's how you had to analyze your business and ensure you'd get those niche customers.*

Mike: You know, looking back, there's quite a bit of luck involved. We were already going down the quality path at the time it happened. It accelerated that path and we started getting wins with our contractors. Thank goodness that's the way it went.

Turns out the box stores became a symbol of mediocrity for our contractors. They don't feel very special when they're shopping there. At Dunn, we've got a free cup of coffee and we know them by name, and we provide them with the product and services they need.

Eric: *Mike, the folks reading this book are looking to draw on the experience of successful contractors and successful businesses that have worked in the industry, like you. With all of your years of experience, and having the perspective on the industry that you do, I'm sure you have had many opportuni-*

ties to witness and observe and adsorb the good and bad traits and qualities in contractors that lead to running a successful business, or leading to one that constantly struggles or dies altogether. Can you talk about the good and the bad and give folks an idea about what things you've consistently seen over the years that make them stand apart?

Mike: Interestingly enough, I think it's sad but true, many times the very best craftsmen are not the best contracting businesses. A lot of it has to do with the way they approach their communication, the way they market their product and the way they promote themselves.

I wouldn't want to say that the successful guys aren't good craftsmen. In fact, I'm sure in many cases they are very good craftsmen, but that element of communication and the ability to deal with the expectations of a customer who has looked in a magazine, seen a picture and imagined their house in a certain way and imagine the budget they have is going to cover that.

Dealing with those expectations is a greater task than doing the remodel itself. Unless you've addressed that, you're going to have disappointment. When you've done your best work with what you have to deal with and with the budget you've been given and that customer is still disappointed, unfortunately you're the one to blame.

You've got to make sure their expectations are in line with reality. If they aren't, you'd be better to walk away from the job and tell them they're probably not going to be happy with it, than to go forward hoping they're going to be happy because likely they're not. Those are actually the stories I hear and actually the experience I've had personally with contractors that were in my own house.

Secondly, the communication continues after the job has begun. If the homeowner wants to upgrade and add things to the job, it's very easy for that budget to get out of control, and then there's the disappointment of running out of money before the job is done or getting the bill that is way more than you expect. I think that dealing with the communication is probably the key issue.

At Dunn Lumber, we always like to say we under promise and over deliver. When we're sure the product is going to be here Tuesday, we say Wednesday by the latest. If we can deliver it by Tuesday, we've made a friend. If we promise by Tuesday and we don't get it out, we've failed, and that customer is going to hold us to that.

The last thing is in terms of building those relationships and making sure that that customer is going to be your advocate in the marketplace. That word-of-mouth advertising... you can't buy advertising that's as good as that.

When that Christmas party in that remodeled house happens and everybody oohs and ahhs, that customer is either going to say, "You know it was a great experience. Bob's Remodeling showed us what it was going to cost, they told us how long it was going to take, they showed us pictures of what it was going to look like and they followed through and this is what we got and we're so happy!" or they're going to say that it looks great, but the process was a nightmare!! And that's not what you want.

Eric: *It's so true. So, I want to back up just a tiny bit here. This is really good, Mike, and what I'm hearing you say, if I could summarize, is communicate and manage expectations. Without naming names or going into specifics, when you've experienced contractors that have really expertly managed* *expectations over the years, what does that look like? Do they have a certain way they speak to customers? Do they have a certain manner about them? Can you speak to that a little bit?*

Mike: Well, I had a couple of personal experiences. One was a kitchen remodel where the presentation of the initial meeting, the discussion of products to be used as so forth was very well done. The presentation of the cost was very well done.

But then, during the project, the communication stopped. The person that was in charge of laying out the program was not the person that was doing the work. The person that was doing the work was not a good communicator at all. He was a good carpenter, but he didn't see it as his responsibility to communicate on a regular basis.

When it's your house, you want to know what's going on. "Why are these boxes here? Why did no one come today? Why did you paint that wall and not the rest of the walls?" You know, when you're in the dentist chair, it's nice when the dentist tells you he's going to do something that makes a lot of noise but it really doesn't do anything. It's just kind of a grinding sound, just cleaning the surface of the tooth. So, when you hear that sound you don't wonder if he's tearing your mouth to shreds.

With your house, you care about your house and you want someone to hold your hand. You want someone to look at the projects through your eyes and realize that this is a frightening, risky experience that has to do with where I live, and my family, and I want to know what's going on during the process.

Eric: *Yeah, I think that's a great insight to it. I remember shortly after college, taking part in a course through an employer on some presentation* *skills and this presenter was teaching us some very simple mind maps for making a presentation. He said, "If you remember nothing else, remember this: If you're making a presentation or a speech of some kind, you're always going to be most effective if you'll do it in three parts: First, tell 'em what you're going to tell 'em; second, tell 'em; and third, tell 'em what you told 'em." I thought of that while you were describing that. That's what you need to do with your customers, isn't it?*

Mike: Yes.

Eric: *'Here's what the project is going to look like, here's what it's going to cost, here are the steps we're going to take.' Then, as those steps are going to be taken, narrate the process, which is the communication piece. At the end, summarize and pull their expectations in line with where things have culminated, so everybody walks away happy.*

Mike: You know, the other thing that comes to mind here is that you have to tailor your presentation and your communication to the preferences of your customer. If your customer is an e-mail person, it would be better if you e-mailed. If someone wants to see you face-to-face, you have to make some provision for that. My experience is that contractors have a way they want to communicate and they expect that customer to follow that, and often that's not going to work as well.

Eric: *Exactly. Let's talk about marketing for a minute, Mike. What have you found to be some of the more effective and successful means of marketing? You mentioned this a little while ago and I think you're right on, the absolute best thing you can do is have happy customers. You come in on budget or under budget, communicate well and get it done on time and you're going to* *get referrals. I want to try to help out not only the established contractor, but also the guy that's in his first or second year and has some happy customers, but not a lot of them. He needs to do some more traditional marketing or even some Guerrilla marketing, and maybe doesn't have a background in that and doesn't quite know where to go or what to do. What advice do you have there?*

Mike: Well, it sure seems like today it would be tough to do it without some kind of web presence. You could probably do that as simply as having a good Facebook page.

You're going to need some high quality pictures of your projects and some good narrative to go along with that. You know, you could probably hire a high school kid who has a Facebook account who could put that together for you. I know my son's Facebook page looks like it's professionally done because he takes a lot of pride in it. That would be a great way to get some pictures out.

The second thing I would do is, I'd buy my lumber at a lumber yard rather than at a home center and I'd make friends with a particular guy, at least to start with. I'd find the guy that had been there for a while and I'd do my best to impress him with my work. I'd invite him to my job, I'd bring some pictures in, I'd give him some referrals.

Make him comfortable with your work because he's going to get questions. Homeowners are going to come in there, look at the displays, and ask who can do that for them. I'd make sure he knew that I was hungry for work and I'd make that customer happy and I'd be sure I did. When he sends me somebody, I'd be sure they were happy and maybe I'd offer him a little discount for the ability to take some pictures of the project and post them on my website and for them to give me referrals. "I'm new in the business and I'd like to give you a little discount. If you're happy with the work and you'd be willing to tell others about it…"

Once again, you're just promoting that organic marketing. I don't think you can make it above the noise. I don't think that flyers left on doors or stuffed into newspapers are particularly effective. It doesn't look very professional.

People are so inundated with very high quality marketing that anything less is pretty tough to compete with. It would be better to find either other professionals, plumbers, electricians and so forth, that would give you referrals, the guy at the lumber yard, the Facebook referrals, that would be the way to start.

Eric: *That's a great idea. You're so right, I think, with regard to the more traditional marketing. Back in the day, if you received a brochure or a flyer, or something that was glossy and professionally designed and just looked really sharp, you instantly, whether consciously or not, thought to yourself that that must be a pretty successful company because they spent a lot of money on the design and printing.*

That's no longer the case. Now, professionally done marketing materials are within reach of just about any kind of budget. So, just because somebody gives you something glossy and nicely done doesn't necessarily mean the quality of work that they're going to give you is going to be in line with that.

So, I think you're right. You have to get above that and like you say, show off the actual work that you've done. Make sure it's good work and build some relationships.

That's one other path I want to go down briefly. What other relation-ships do you think are important for contractors to have that are potential sources of referrals? For instance, one of the contractors I've spoken with says that much of the business that he's seen come his way over the years has been from architects.

Mike: There's a lot of design people out there now that are interior designers who aren't architects, who are working with homeowners and doing basic designs of kitchens and baths, etc., where a lot of actual architectural drawings aren't necessary. You're more looking for detail drawings.

So, let's see, the professional designers? You may be able to find that kind of relationship down at the Design Center. I'm not sure how you develop that. Some friends of ours are always looking for someone that will do a good job of turning their ideas into reality, so that would be hugely important.

Eric: *Wonderful. So, let's shift over into this last stage here on the more personal side. You know, you're the president of a large company. You've got a lot of people that are reporting to you, either directly or indirectly. You obviously have to keep yourself pretty sharp, from a leadership standpoint. Can you talk about some of the things like personal development through reading or whatever you're involved in, to mentors, etc. Talk about what you believe is the importance of those sorts of things that may have parallels for contractors, and some of the suggestions you would have for somebody that wants to develop themselves as a leader, business person or entrepreneur.*

Mike: Well, the two things that come to mind are that there are things that your business needs and there are things that *you* need. I can think of some real light bulb moments.

I hired a coach early on that worked for the Blanchard Company. Actually, she'd been an acquaintance and I tracked her down in Arizona, but the coaching all happened over the telephone. The nice thing about hiring a professional coach over someone who is just willing to mentor you is that they're going to say the hard things a little more quickly with a little less cringe because you're paying them to do it. Often it's the hard things they have to say that are the most important.

I remember I had recognized that Dunn Lumber was in the transition days. We were so light on top-end leadership that we really were stuck. We didn't have the breadth of leadership and managers to even buy another location, much less expand in other ways.

I was discussing this with a friend that started his own business a couple of times successfully and he recommended a book called The E-Myth Revisited.

The entrepreneurial myth is that entrepreneurs start businesses, which is in fact not really the case. Most of the time, it's the carpenter that starts the contracting business. He has technical skills of a carpenter but doesn't necessarily have the skills in a business.

In fact, we often see very good skilled people that have gone from working for a company to starting their own business and then transitioning back to working for somebody because the stress that they experienced not having those skills was so great that it was a relief to get back to working for someone again and doing what they love, which was building.

The E-Myth Revisited talks about turning your business into a franchisable model, quantifying and describing and putting down on paper what your business does, how it does it, the structure and guiding principles. Then just accumulating the best practices. If you know that Christmas lands on a Friday, what days do you take off?

What we were finding was that we were making those decisions on the fly all the time. More than half of our time was taken up just keeping up on all these types of decisions. Once you have everything written down you can actually start giving your time to more important things, like where are you going and what's going to happen next year and how you want to grow.

Personally, a lot of times what you need is for someone to tell you that 'Your intention is "this" and I see that you want it with all of your might, but your impact on the way you're going about it is negative, and that's why you're having these results.'

Learning the difference between intention and impact was probably the biggest light bulb moment in my life, and that happened probably 20 years ago. My father and my uncle took me into the back room and said, "You know, you are perceived as a very angry person. You're good at what you do and you want to do well, but when you talk to others they think you're mad at them and nobody wants to talk to you."

That was really devastating at the time because I was working really hard, and it was just my desire to do a great job that was producing these emotions. But I realized I had to approach it in a completely different way and I started working with a coach at that time and just working on how I was presenting myself, and that made a huge difference.

I guess to summarize the two things that your business needs, it needs the basic structure, practices, procedures. It needs those quantified, and everyone needs to understand them and needs to understand what your values are and what's important for the business and how you go about things.

Secondly, professionally, you need to know how to present those things in a way that people can hear; the way that you intend them to hear it and it needs to be a consistent, positive message. It can't be the flavor of the week. It can't be "It's this when he's happy and this when he's mad." It has to be consistent because that builds trust and the way that you treat those employees is the way they're going to treat your customers. It has to be a consistent value system from your vendors, to your employees, to your customers, or it's not going to be a consistent message and you're not going to build that trust.

Eric: *I think that's absolutely wonderful, Mike. As I see it, you were really lucky, and you probably agree, that your father and uncle cared enough to take you in the back room and share that with you. All of us need that and a few of us get it, right? I guess you have to just ask someone that's close to you how you're perceived as a boss, a manager… I know I do it with my kids. I want to know if I'm being the kind of Dad they want me to be and I won't know it unless I ask them. So, what's your barometer after having gone through that experience? Do you seek feedback from your employees or from those that took you aside, or both?*

Mike: Well, just as you said that, I can think of four people I'm pretty close to who will walk in, shut the door and say, "I don't know how you came across right there, but it wasn't very positive."

That's invaluable and you have to reward people for giving you that kind of information. If you don't have those types of people, you can hire them. You can hire a coach, you can bring them into your business and you can allow them to watch you operate. They can do a 360 review where they go around to all the people around you and take a survey of how you're perceived.

I've done that, too, and it's very helpful. If you're a tyrant and those people won't even be truthful on 360, that's probably going to become pretty obvious to a coach when they come into that work. They're going to sense that oppressive spirit in your business. They're going to know right away, but if you're that kind of person, you're probably not asking for feedback anyway. If you're worried about it and you want to know, you're probably already on the right path for finding out.

Eric: *So true. Well Mike, two last things. First, if you're in the shoes of a contractor looking to get it going, what books do you recommend?*

Mike: You know, the three books that we ask all of our employees to read are The E Myth, Good to Great and the Seven Habits of Highly Successful People.

The E Myth is about where we're going as a business, why we're doing the best practice thing and why it's important. Good to Great is about principle centered planning. We have our values that underlie everything we do. We're seeking to always be consistent with those values and at every new hire orientation I explain what those values are, and I tell our employees that they can interact with our values on three levels. They can ignore them, in which case they won't be around for very long. They can abide by them and they can stay their whole career with us. Or, they can actually engage with them to teach others and to help us become more consistent and they'll rise to leadership.

Then, the Seven Habits is really about effectiveness. Effective habits of organization, or thinking ahead, envisioning an end and making plans to reach it, or creating synergy with others, those are great principles.

Eric: *When you were describing a few things from E Myth I was actually* *thinking of Seven Habits, which is a book that has had one of the greatest impacts on my life and career. I was thinking of the quadrant, and you were referring to those things that you guys have spent so much time over the years reacting to when really they were urgent, but not terribly important. Once you created the system that made those things take care of themselves, it frees up time to focus on those non-urgent, but highly important things.*

Mike: Let me really stress, I've said a lot of things that sound like we've got it all figured out. We've been using those principles and applying them every day. One of the things that we were just talking about with our managers is that if you have a philosophy of constant improvement, that means you constantly need to improve, and it's not always easy to continue the phrase.

I've been in this business for 40 years. I have a lot to learn, I have a lot of room to grow and I have to be willing to look at my failures on a regular basis or I'm not going to be improving. Sometimes our managers, when they've been around for 20 years, think they have it figured out and want to know why we keep bugging them. It's a matter of continuous growth. That's what makes life exciting.

Eric: *Absolutely. I'm not sure who to attribute this to because I think I've heard it from various speakers and authors, but the essence of the quote is "if you're not growing, you're dying." It's one or the other and you're either advancing or retreating, there is no standing still. If you think you're just maintaining, you're not. You're likely moving backward.*

Well Mike, I'm going to put you on the spot. In a few sentences, what's your advice for a guy that's sitting across from you that asks for a few nuggets about how to have a successful career in business?

Mike: Well, you know, I think it was Tom Peters that was always saying "Find something that you love doing and do it with all your might." A lot of times that's why contractors are in the business. They love building something, they love producing something beautiful.

I think that you have to make sure nothing stands in the way of that and you have to communicate, like we've said, along with the process. You present your vision to someone; let them join in with that vision and help shape it.

Then you communicate how you're doing it along the way and make sure that it's in line with those expectations and that the customer is moving along with you in it, and then you present the final product. You feel good about getting the price that you asked for and then you continue to take that project forward, in pictures, in recommendation, in reputation, and you do it again.

It's pretty simple, but it's hard to do. It's because we get caught in the minutia, we get caught in the disappointment. Periodically, we take a big hit. We use a product that didn't work out the way we expected or fail in some way, or the expectation never really got communicated correctly and we've got to eat it, and that's hard.

You know, that's why you want to partner with a good lumber yard because we often stand with our contractors in just that way and help them make it through those tough times. There have been a lot of times when we've had nothing to do with it, but we shared it three ways. The vendor picked up a third, we picked up a third and the contractor only had to eat a third when he would have had to eat the whole thing.

Eric: *Well, from personal experience, Dunn Lumber is a great company to work with. Once you've been in there a couple of times it's not uncommon for* *them to greet you with a smile and address you by name. We all know that makes you feel special and important when that happens and that's just one of the little things they do to show you that you're important to them.*

So, I applaud Dunn Lumber, and you Mike, for what you guys have done with it. I just hope and pray you'll have continued success and weather this economic storm that we're all part of right now. You guys have obviously been through lots of highs and lows over 103 years and so I just wish you all the best, and I'm so grateful for your contribution here. I just know it's going to be of great value to everybody that's going to take in the information.

Mike: Well, Eric, thank you for the kind words, it was my pleasure.

Paul Moon
Principal | Architect
Paul Moon Design

About Paul

Paul Moon is the owner and principal architect at Paul Moon Design. Paul has been involved in architecture for about 16 years. His firm is involved in mainly high-end residential and landscape architecture, from kitchens and full-scale remodels to new construction.

He lives in Seattle with his wonderful wife and two young daughters, and has built quite an architecture practice.

Paul enjoys soccer, basketball and following his beloved Yankees, 2009's World Series champions.

We are very fortunate to have his insight, as he's had a very successful career and has worked with many general contractors and subcontractors over the years, observing all of the good – and sometimes bad – that they have to offer.

Eric: *Thanks for joining us, Paul.*

Paul: Yes, thank you for having me.

Eric: *Let's dive in. One of the things that most successful contractors know is that having some good relationships with architects is really important, so we'll get into those details today. Why don't you start out by telling us a little about your background though, and how and why you got into architecture, then bring us up to the present.*

Paul: Well, strangely enough, I knew I wanted to be an architect since I was a child and I actually got into it when I was about seven. My father was a dentist and was building his dental practice, a building.

Every day during the summer my father and I would go and meet with the contractors to take a look at the progress and I was just fascinated with how the building went up and the progress of it. I never forgot that.

In high school, we had a great drafting program where we did a lot of hand drafting and I got an opportunity to permit a teacher's house and it just kind of reaffirmed my love for it. So I went up to the University of Washington and got an undergraduate degree in architecture and went to go work for an architect that was in the area doing residential additions and remodels.

It was a small office and back before the computer drafting, so I got a chance to hand draft and do a little answering of phones and fixing the blueprint machine; a little bit of everything. I worked at a few different firms over the years and then in 2001 I decided to go out on my own.

Eric: *That's great. What has that been like, going out on your own?*

Paul: You know, it's been great. It certainly was a challenge. It was difficult getting started and took a lot of time and patience to build up my clientele, but I'm in my tenth year now and things feel like they are healthy and I've built a good client base and I get some great projects.

Eric: *That's pretty awesome—you actually knew when you were a kid that you wanted to be an architect. I think most folks would probably envy that. The typical boy wants to be a football player, a police officer or a fireman, maybe a pilot. But, few actually know exactly what they want to be and end up pursuing that later in life.*

So, talk a bit about your practice, how it has evolved over the years, what sort of projects you typically work on. What are your favorite and least favorite parts of the business?

Paul: You bet. Well, first of all, I must say, one of my lifelong dreams was to be center fielder for the Yankees, too, but I realized fairly early on that that wasn't going to happen.

I'll tell you a little bit about how I started the business. One of the things I noticed is that the typical way an architect starts their own practice is by working at a larger firm first and develop a relationship with clients and someone says perhaps, "Why don't you design my house?" The architect looks at it and says "Wow, that could be a few months worth of income. I'll get this project, do a good job and then use the same amount of time that I'm working on it to go find a couple more."

What I've also seen a few times is that if some work doesn't come, that person is forced to go back to the big firms. I took a different strategy, that in order to build my portfolio and build references, I took anything and everything at the start.

I started out designing decks, bathrooms and basement re-models. Basically, anything that anybody would trust me with, and my philosophy was that if I could have 20 references after my first year instead of having one then I'd have 20 people talking about me and recommending me to friends.

So, I kind of went with a bottom up approach to building the type of projects that I like. It took a few years, but slowly someone would say, "Okay, you did a great job on a basement, here's a kitchen remodel," and "You did a great job on a kitchen remodel, here's an addition." Then, "You did a great job on an addition, here's a new house."

It took me a few years, but I got to the point where I could get the confidence from my clients and their references that they felt comfortable recommending me to most types of residential. My main focus has been residential architecture.

After doing different building types, I really enjoy residential architecture because of how personal it is with the families. You get to really be a part of their family and recognize their dreams, their dream house.

The project duration is usually very short. I'm usually with them about a year and a half from the time we start designing to construction. The construction type is something that's fairly easy to understand, the wood frame construction. So, I've chosen to focus on the residential architecture.

Eric: *That's great, Paul. I want to go down that path here in a second, but before I do, I want to touch back on something. I think that was really smart the approach you took to getting your business off the ground and it sounds like in looking back you probably wouldn't do things much differently because it's helped you to grow your practice more efficiently and quicker than you could have otherwise, without the pressure of having to go back to the big firm to stay afloat.*

Talk about it, if you would, because I think there are a lot of contractors reading this that are in a similar position with their business. They are small and would like to have a little more stability, grow their business... We've talked with contractors all across the board, some that are relatively new in their careers and some that have been doing it for decades.

Of course, the ones that have been in it for many years are in a position now where they don't have to do a lot of marketing because they do have a lot of successful projects behind them and happy clients behind them. But, when you're starting out you don't have that. So, I think the approach you took was really smart and one that a lot of contractors, early on in their careers, could follow.

Talk about how you were intentional about going out and getting those first, say, 20 projects in that first year, versus the one or two big ones. What are some ways you marketed yourself and got the word out?

Paul: Well, I think the first step was letting people know that I was on my own and was ready to help them. That was a matter of letting friends, family and colleagues know.

Even though you're a small company, you can present yourself like a big company and you should run yourself like a big company. Try to get yourself an e-mail that reflects your business name, or some letterhead, just present a professional appearance.

Then I think you go through a phase where people run into you, socially or what not, and ask what you're doing nowadays and you've got to get that word out.

I know one of things that I tried initially that had some mixed success, was that I had some real estate lists and I targeted neighborhoods I'd liked to do some designs in. That wasn't great success but it did get my name out and maybe that was something that made people familiar with my business name.

I also found that if you do things socially, with your community, church or at sporting events, just networking with people you know, letting them know that no job is too small and you're willing to try stuff. That's primarily what I did to get started.

I also made sure, at that starting phase, that I didn't take anything that was over my head. I think that's critical because you have to treat each job at that phase as a golden opportunity to get more jobs and more references and you really can't screw one of those up in the sense where someone's not happy with you because the amount of people you have is too fragile and so limited at that stage.

So I think one of the keys is recognizing when someone is talking about how they have a whole new house to do, I might have said that I'd refer them to a friend, or partner up with someone, a bigger firm to do that.

Eric: *That's great advice. I think you nailed it right on. Paul, one of the things I'd like to talk about that I think will be very helpful to folks is your perspective on contractors. I want to talk about the good and bad things* *you've experienced over the years and what makes for a good relationship with a contractor.*

Before we do, to kind of start that off, there's this triangular relationship with you, the client and the contractor. I know that sometimes the client comes to you already knowing the builder that they want to work with and then you handle the design. But I also know a lot of times they don't have a builder chosen and are looking to you for guidance there. Talk about that and if you could take a stab at the percentages of how often a client comes to you with a builder in mind and how often your recommendation is sought out.

Paul: Sure. I would say 80% of the time the client does not have a builder when they come to me. That's why I think it's so important for builders to have good relationships with architects.

The other 20% is when one of the builders I've worked with in the past has usually recommended me for the job because we have a good working relationship and he's using me to help get the job, selling us as a good team because that client recognizes the value of a good team.

Over the years, I've developed a list of contractors I've enjoyed working with and I categorized them sometimes into separate geographic areas or project types. Some contractors may not work in a certain area because it's remote, other contractors are great at doing certain types of projects, but not others.

Regardless, I think it's important for a builder to know that one of the most difficult things in the project is the budget. Initially, whether I tell the client what I think it's going to cost or the builder does, I think the client is surprised with how much it costs.

There tends to be sometimes a distrust of the initial number so I usually tell the contractors that I work with that we're going to do a preliminary design on a project and I'm going to be bringing two or three of you in to interview and it's going to be up to the client who they decide to choose.

But, the key to that process is if all three of them give good numbers, and your references and budgets, the client will then, whoever they select, feel comfortable with your numbers because they've seen two others and that will validate their price. They'll feel you've given a fair price and done their research and I think that helps the relationship throughout the project.

Eric: *I would imagine another benefit for you is that if for some reason there are problems later it has saved you from a lot of risk in having brought the only contractor to the table that they're unhappy with.*

Paul: Yes, and I think it comes down into our business where contractors and architects are the same way, especially in residential architecture; this is going to be the largest transaction the clients will have done in their lives.

They're a little bit scared, a little bit nervous, a little bit hesitant. Maybe they don't visualize very well and maybe don't understand what things cost. So this whole process is about showing them their options and their choices and getting them to the point where they feel comfortable.

Some people want to talk to five contractors and some people say that whoever I want to work with they're comfortable with. It's reading people and getting them to the point where they trust you because there are so many times in this process when you're building the project where they really don't know what's going on and you have to say, "Just trust me that this is going to be okay."

Eric: *Yes, trust is so important. I think you're right; for clients it's not only about the financial investment, but like you said earlier, they're envisioning their dream of what this project is going to look like. Whether it's a new home from the ground up or a complete remodel, there's that fear factor of 'What if when it's finished it's not everything I've dreamed of?' There's a fear there of making any mistakes or bad choices that might cloud that.*

So Paul, one of the things I'd like you to address is that there are a lot of folks reading this who aren't home builders, they are specialty contractors or subcontractors or remodelers and they might be thinking, 'Okay, what value is there in this for me in having a relationship with architects? I'm not looking to have clients referred to me that want to build a home.' How often do you get calls from clients asking to get a deck built or a bathroom remodeled that don't need design work, but are looking for someone that can help. Do you get many of those calls?

Paul: I do. I do a lot, and I actually keep a database of all the good subcontractors that I've worked with, in addition to the contractors.

There's two things I'd say that are relevant. One, I get a lot of calls for electricians and plumbers and drywallers from homeowners or clients or friends, and it's always important for me to recommend someone good.

When I'm on the jobsite, when I find someone that is good with people and clean and does good work, that's someone that I catalog.

Another thing, I'll give you an example, is let's say that I'm working on project that has a lot of very difficult finish concrete and a lot of it's going to be exposed and very visible. The general contractor that I'm working with may have a great concrete subcontractor that can do this no problem and the job turns out beautiful.

But, down the line, I may be working someplace else, in another city or different area with a different general contractor and I have to do a similar type project, but they don't have a finish subcontractor for concrete. I often will say, "Try giving this person a call. They did a beautiful job for me." Those generals know that if it made the architect happy that takes one off their list and they're willing to give it a try.

Eric: *That's great. Okay, so that's a good segue; there are two additional topics I want to cover here. Please talk about what a successful project looks like from the standpoint of your relationship with the contractor and go into the elements that leave you with a good taste in your mouth about having worked with that contractor, which is going to ensure there's a good possibility you'll refer him in the future and that the client's going to be happy, because you'll be affirming that choice to the client, which can only lead to good things after that.*

So talk about what a successful project looks like from that standpoint and some of the traits and behaviors and actions that you witness in a contractor that does a great job pleasing you and the homeowner. Actually, that's a mouthful, so I'll jump to the next question I had after you finish that.

Paul: I guess the bottom line is that a successful relationship is at the end of the project when the construction is done and the client says, "You guys were great!"; and my unofficial metric for how well we did is if we get invited over for dinner. If we get invited over for dinner by the client then that means they liked us. If we don't, then maybe we have some questions to ask.

But, to break it down, there are different parts of the process. The first part is, when I introduce you to the client you're able to prepare a budget that's fairly detailed and as architects, we tend to do very specific drawings. I not only have drawings, but I've invested a lot of time in design and I've gone to different showrooms with the client. I'll have a list of specifications of materials.

So, the first step is for the contractor to price what I've specified and give a realistic budget. Now, if we get through that budget part, we get the contract, and a good contractor during the pre-construction phase for me is someone who is always looking to be budget conscience.

Someone who is always coming back to me with some alternate materials that might save some money, or some alternate ways of doing things, always asking questions. Making sure that by the time we get the contract, that price that they give is going to hold firm during construction.

I think that one of the single most important things is, often times it will take me 4 -6 months to get the drawings and the permitting done with all of the interior finishes and everything. That's a lot of time for a contractor to double check; bring subs out to the project.

To me, it's very important to the client that once we start construction with our project and our project team, you're not going to see a bunch of change orders and price increases during construction unless they're initiated by the client changing things.

Now, I think another thing during construction that's important is communication and timeliness. On our projects the contractor will typically furnish a schedule and a calendar for us to follow.

Any time there might be change orders they are written and sent ahead of time. We'll typically have weekly meetings on the jobsite to discuss outstanding items, upcoming items, things that we need to decide in the next little bit. That communication, along with the billings that usually come monthly, are clear and reflect that work done.

Then at the end, it's finishing up strong in terms of the punch list. One of the things contractors often neglect to do is allow somewhat of a budget for all of the little bumps and dings and things that the clients notice at the end. They're usually small things, but the contractors I've had less luck with don't get back to the client or don't fix those things. They may have done a great job for 95% of the project, but it's that last 5% that the client remembers and the client comes back with an average recommendation.

I very much look at the contractor and me as a team during construction, and for me to be able to recommend somebody again and do it again, the client has to say that the contractor was great. Sometimes someone could say that Paul Moon Design doesn't have a great list of contractors to work with and that would hurt my recommendation, so it's finishing up strong and coming back for those call backs and making sure that the client, when you give them the keys and they move in, are really happy.

Eric: *Yes, that's great. Clear communication and follow-up are so big and unfortunately seem to be two biggest areas that contractors fall short.*

Paul: And Eric, just to follow up with that, I'd say it's a very simple list: 1. Get your job done on budget; 2. Get your job done on time; and 3. Communicate.

I'd almost say that the 'communicate' is more important. Some of the good contractors I work with put everything that they can into the punch list and final paint touch ups because some people's idea of what a good contractor is, is how good the paint job is, because in the end that's something that everybody sees at the dinner party.

I've had numerous clients say, "Well can we save some money by painting ourselves?" and I've had a couple contractors say, "There's one thing I won't let you do is paint because everybody sees that and they're going to think that's a reflection of my quality of work."

So, it's those three things and sometimes doing the quality of the work isn't as important as the communication and follow-up.

Eric: *Great advice, Paul. So, to wrap up, somebody reading this should be convinced by now that having solid relationships with some good architects can be very key to building your business, whatever your area of specialty is. But, if I'm starting out or I might even have an established business but have never really gone that route, can you give some advice and suggestions as to how a contractor could begin seeking out and cultivating some of those relationships?*

Talk about some of the ways that contractors have introduced themselves to you, or marketed themselves to you. And whether that has happened or not, talk about some of the ways you as an architect would be receptive to contractor marketing. I want contractors to walk away from this feeling like they have a good idea of some things they could start doing today to build this part of their business.

Paul: Well, I think that for the contractors out there, what they need to know about architects is that architects want a builder that executes their design.

One of the red flags for me in terms of a contractor out there, is a lot of contractors like to design, too. I think it's important for the contractor, when they're starting or establishing their business, is to decide if they are going to be someone that likes to design/build and walk the client through finishes.

There are a lot of husband and wife teams, for example, where the wife does the interior design and the material selection in some of the books and then the husband builds. Those are very difficult kinds of relationships for the architect because the architect doesn't want to get in a discussion on site about granite countertops or the color of the paint when they may have dealt with the client for a long time.

I would say, if you're going to pursue architects, let them know that you're open to the cookbook approach, which is "You give me the instructions and I'm going to build it the way you want it."

So I would say having some photos of millwork or cabinets or certain details you've done on projects that were unique to show that you can pull them off. That may work.

I would also say, every builder that I've ever met I've been introduced to through a client, where the client says he wants you to try this contractor, and in the end they've selected them, and after working with them I've really enjoyed working with them and I've recommended them jobs.

If you're breaking in and wanted to market to a few architects I would say maybe a nice flyer that goes out to them, a phone call to them that says you'd really like to build your business through architects and that you know how important that relationship is.

If you find some architects that you think you could work with, because I think that's just as important because not all architects are going to be easy to work with, I think the most important marketing would be to bring them a project.

Find a small project that maybe doesn't need too much design, or whatever is comfortable in your scope of work. Tell them you want to bring this to them and that you want this to be the project you try things out on. Maybe it's not too big to start out with and then you see how things go from there.

Eric: *That's a really interesting viewpoint. It dawned on me as you were saying that - maybe an angle for a contractor to take would be to do some research, identify a handful of architects that you'd really like to work with, and then maybe do some marketing to your own personal contacts.*

Tell your contacts that if they have a project in mind that they'd like to pursue but haven't yet talked with an architect, that you have a few really good ones that you might be able to recommend to them. Then, rustle up some business for those architects so you don't have to come empty-handed. That's always a great start to a relationship if you can bring something to the table versus coming with your empty hands outstretched.

Paul: Yeah, and I think that that's a good strategy, because maybe 8 out of 10 clients come to me not having a builder, and if someone has a big new beautiful house they want to design chances are I'm not going to use someone I haven't worked with before. I want to use the contractor that I know is going to be a home run that we're going to get those characteristics we talked about.

I think a great way to break in with these architects would be someone that goes in and brings them a project, ready to start out small, see how your systems work and then move on from there.

Another thing I think is important, too, is a number of times I've found these relationships with these builders and they've started on small jobs. Then, the next job we get a little bit bigger and bigger and we get to the larger projects.

My philosophy is to start small and build it up and make sure we can pull off each level of the project and then find my "A" list of contractors that can pull off my "A" list of projects.

Sometimes what has happened is that architects get word of a good builder that's just starting out doing a great job on these small projects and two or three architects refer them for bigger jobs and then sometimes things blow up on the contractor because they get too busy and they don't have the infrastructure to be able to handle the paperwork.

Three or four jobs may be running at the same time and they end up ruining their references with both the clients and the architects. I've had that happen before, so I think that's something to be careful of, too.

That goes back to when I initially started my business, the philosophy of 'only take what you can handle and don't say yes to things over your head', and I think people respect that when a builder is having success and growing but says he can't handle that many at a time but is working on staffing up for it.

Eric: *I think you're right. When a contractor, or any professional, turns down business with the reasoning that they're just not equipped to handle it, knowing how badly most companies want and need business, I think when somebody comes to you in that fashion it certainly builds a lot of trust and speaks volumes with regard to integrity. If it doesn't work out, now you certainly end up thinking that that is somebody you want to work with in the future.*

So, Paul, if you would, give us your final words of wisdom. For the folks that are reading, whether they're getting started, they're small and want to get bigger, be more successful, more profitable, build their business, at whatever size or level they're at, give us a few gems for them to walk away with to feel equipped to go out and start growing.

Paul: I would say the overall key to me is: build your business honestly. I think everyone knows there are right ways and wrong ways to do things.

I think in this business there are a million contractors, a million subcontractors, a million architects, and you have to provide some kind of value to your client. That value is being organized. That value is finding good deals and presenting good options to people, getting the job done on time and being sort of a people pleaser. I think it's good if people take things slowly, don't try to build too fast.

One thing we haven't covered here is cash flow. I've seen a lot of contractors purchase a lot of trucks and equipment and things too early and get saddled with debt where they have to take on more jobs that maybe get over their head, or too many at a time.

Take it slow. Do a good job for everyone. Ask for references. Decide what type of contractor you want to be. Do you want to be a subcontractor that markets to general contractors? Do you want to be a contractor that gets most of their work from architects, or do you like working directly with homeowners?

So if you know who you are and have a clear vision for your company and take it a step at a time where you know you're profitable at each step, I think it's a formula for success.

Eric: *That's wonderful. Paul, thank you so much for taking the time, and I know this is going to be tremendously valuable for all those contractors that are reading this and really were curious and perhaps confused and not sure where to go with regard to building their business with architects. For those of you that are reading, if you ever do need to work with a professional architect, Paul is one of the best. If you ever have a client that isn't working with one, I* *encourage you to make contact with Paul. Paul's website is www.paulmoondesign.com. Thanks again, Paul, I sure appreciate it.*

Paul: You bet, thank you.

Dave Taylor
Owner | Agent
Taylor Insurance

About Dave

Dave Taylor is an insurance agent with Farmers Insurance. He's been with Farmer's for 22 years. He's been in insurance, and with Farmers, for his entire professional career, which is pretty noteworthy.

Dave is in the top 1% of Farmers agents in the country (out of thousands) and Farmers is one of the top insurance companies in the world. He's just about as successful as they come in this field, so we're very lucky to have him here.

Some reading this may be wondering why I would interview an insurance agent. The reason is that Dave has a very unique perspective on the industry. Over the years, he has had many, many clients who are contractors. Dave has thousands of clients at this point and many of them are contractors who have been with him for years.

Dave has the unique perspective of really getting to observe the intricacies and best practices of successful contractors. And, of course, he's also seen a lot of things that don't work, and we're going to talk about both.

We also are going to talk about the fact that as a business owner and someone who had his own office building built, he has been involved in many real estate investment transactions and projects where he has been in different roles in construction projects.

He's had a lot of interactions with contractors and a lot of interaction with the different parties that play a part in construction projects. He brings a wealth of knowledge and a lot of insight that we're lucky to glean from him.

Last, but not least, we're also going to talk with him about some of the things he's done, and some of the different things that have helped him to be successful in his career, which work for just about any other industry when it comes to being successful and as it pertains to personal development.

Eric: *Dave, thanks so much for being with us today, I really appreciate it.*

Dave: You're welcome!

Eric: *So, where we typically start, Dave, is we'd love to hear about your background. Tell us how you got started in the insurance industry and when and why, and kind of give us a review of your career with Farmers and bring us up to the present.*

Dave: Okay, well I want to say thank you, Eric, for allowing me this opportunity and I do hope there's some information that I can share with you and your readers that would be of value.

For me, going back to when I graduated from High School, I wasn't sure what I wanted to do. I thought I knew but didn't have the resources to pay for four years of education and then find out I didn't want to do that, so I joined the Marine Corp.

I served in the Marine Corp. for a few years before I then went off to college and was studying to be an electrical engineer. I discovered I didn't enjoy that. I tried accounting and didn't enjoy that.

Then one summer, between school years, I did an accounting internship for a Farmers Insurance agent and I really fell in love with what he did. I liked the idea of owning my own business. I liked the idea of having different challenges every day, meeting with different clients, interacting with the people... There were so many things about what he was doing that I was drawn to.

I actually dropped out of college and immediately became a Farmers agent, and that was 22 years ago. So, it's been a full career already and I enjoy it immensely.

The way that I run my agency has changed quite a bit over that 22 year period. When I first started we were primarily what you'd call a personal lines agency doing homes and autos and life insurance, and stayed that way for about the first eight years.

Then, in about that 8th or 9th year I was exposed to the commercial side of the business and really was taken by that and the challenges that it offered.

The opportunities to work with business owners were a lot more challenging than what we call the order taking side of our business, which is doing the autos and homes. So from that point on we really hit it hard with the commercial side and that's become probably 65-70% of our agency now. We have a staff of 5-6, depending on when it is, but 5 or 6 full-time individuals here. Like I said, the bulk of what we do now is commercial. Of the commercial work, I'd say that 40% of that is representative of contractors. We have a lot of contractors insured, so hopefully we can add something here today that would be of value.

Eric: *Yes, absolutely. Now, a quick question regarding that route you took of really having the majority of your business mix be on the commercial side. What percentage of agents, would you say, structure their business that way?*

Dave: You know, I'll speak specifically to what I know the best, which is Farmers, but I think it's going to be fairly representative of the rest of the industry as well. Within Farmers, in the state that I'm in, there are 750 agents and out of those 750 there are probably ten that I would say follow that same model of attempting to really be a commercial agency that also accommodates personal lines. So, the percentage may be less than 5%.

Eric: *I would guess that the reason for that is it's probably a tough business to build, and you mentioned that when you first went that route you were attracted to the challenge of that. Obviously you did it successfully and have really bolstered that and have grown it over the years. To what would you attribute the success of building the commercial side of your business?*

Dave: You're right on as far as why more people don't do it; it's very challenging. On the personal lines, auto and home side of our business, it's pretty cookie cutter. You only have a few different coverage options and it's really the same scenario almost every single time you look at it.

When you go to the commercial side it's just complicated right off the bat, depending on what type of business entity it is and then what type of business it is as well. Even within that, if it's a contractor, what type of contractor?

So there's just so many different variables before you even get to the coverages, which are pretty complicated as well. So it's a steep learning curve and a lot of agents just don't have the patience to learn, or the time to learn, and they need to get out there and make money quickly so they stick to what's easy.

As far as what I attribute the success of our agency to, I think there are a few things. I think we were fortunate to stumble into commercial at about that 8 or 9 year mark. I had a client that kind of dragged me into commercial and asked me to help him out. So being pulled into it, first of all, was very fortunate and I feel blessed that it happened.

Secondly, there's a certain discipline and structure required for commercial that I think we have a lot of systems in place for here in our agency and those systems have helped us be successful.

Another thing is, I feel we have the best staff of any of the agencies that I'm aware of. Our staff is top notch and they do a fantastic job and our clients truly appreciate that and we get compliments about it all the time and receive referrals quite a bit. To me that's just a testament to the fact that we're doing a good job on the staffing side. We don't let the balls fall out of the air or let things slip through the cracks. I think all of those things have played a part in it.

Eric: *That's great. So Dave, I know that after this many years you have thousands of clients, so you probably have hundreds, at a minimum, who are contractors. As I said in the introduction, what's great about this is we get to glean some insight from you as being an observer of contractors and in some cases you really get to dive into their financials, and I'd say you almost have a bit of an intimate relationship with a lot of your clients because there is so* *much you have to know to take care of them properly.*

That's the assumption I'm making, but you can expand on that. In addition, what we'd really like to hear and I think would be a lot of value to folks is just hearing about some of your observations over the years of the things you've seen time in and time out with successful contractors, as well as things that you've consistently seen that trip up contractors. Just talk about some of your experiences and observances because you have a unique viewpoint on this.

Dave: Sure. That's a really good question. You know, thinking about that just as you were asking it, there's two things that came to mind right away.

The first one, if we're speaking just specifically about what are the things that successful contractors do that I've worked with and what's made them successful or set them apart, the first one being that almost without exception the successful ones, by the time they get to me, have already thought out their business plan.

They have a business plan. They aren't looking to start business tomorrow. They didn't just quit working for the general contractor yesterday and they want to start their business tomorrow. They've been thinking this through, they have a business plan, they're doing their research or due diligence finding out, okay, what do we need to do? What are the insurance requirements? What's that going to cost us? What are the bonding requirements? They're getting it all laid out in advance and then they have a plan. They treat it like a business.

Quite often what we see happen, and I can probably almost tell you when they walk through the door which ones are going to fail, based on this one point, is that we'll see guys run in the door and they've been a general contractor. Now they've got a buddy that wants a roof done and so they're going to be their own roofing contractor, so they're a technician. They're a roofer, they're not a business owner.

They run into this thing thinking all they're going to do is do roofs and they don't know how to run a business. Those guys are typically gone before their first renewal, so they don't last a full twelve months of their insurance policy.

Then there's the guys who come in and they're running it like a business. Yes, they're the technician, but they're also either the business owner that has a business or they're partnering with someone that's going to help them with that or they've hired it done.

We've seen that in the past, too. We'll have a guy come in with his accountant that he's going to work with and his banker and their different partners. It's the guy that comes in by himself without any business management experience or any plan, he's just going to go out and take the jobs as they come - he's the guy that typically fails.

That's the first thing and then the second thing is, not as important, but important, are the ones that have funding. They're not coming in already broke. That's not to say that those guys don't succeed, sometimes they do, but the guys that have a hard time can't even scrape together the money for the down payment on their insurance and we're calling them every 30 days reminding them that we need to get a payment.

They're robbing Peter to pay Paul, and those guys seem to struggle as well, compared to guys that come in and have a little bit of a bank roll that will at least carry them for the first two or three months while they're getting off the ground. That plays itself out.

Even some of the contractors we have that are still on the books, that are not organized, that are not running their business, they're letting their business run them. Those are the guys that we see are still struggling to this day.

I think about some of my most successful clients and it's a full on business; they have staff that are doing the pieces of the business they don't think they're competent enough to do or they don't' want to deal with and they're doing the stuff they're good at and want to do.

Eric: *It's interesting, Dave, I've spoken with a lot of successful contractors for this book and to go right along with what you were saying, so many of them talk about professionalism and being organized and understanding their business and all those sorts of things, just like you were hitting on. What was also interesting is that Mike Dunn, the president of Dunn Lumber, has all of his employees read a book called "E-Myth Revisited" by Michael Gerber, which is a favorite in my own library. It talks about how a lot of entrepreneurs are often good at a craft, they're good "technicians", but they need to be a business person or entrepreneur also, maybe even primarily, so they can be the painter or the roofer and make a living doing it. Everything you've shared has definitely been backed up by some of the successful contractors I've been talking to.*

Dave: I'd like to echo what Mr. Dunn said. I actually met Michael Gerber about 15 years ago and got a copy of that book from him. That is probably one of the principal books that changed the way I looked at my business and so I couldn't recommend that book highly enough either. It's a quick read, it's a good read and it's very easy to understand. So, I agree; I would say it's a must-read!

Eric: *All right, for all of you reading this, take note. That's the second person who has said you must read that book. (Author's note: I have read E-Myth as well. It is spectacular.)*

So, Dave, let's switch gears a little bit here. One of the things about this book that's a little different from what one might expect, is that it is not just about "How to be a successful contractor". That's the ultimate result and I want it to be of value in that way, but there's a lot that goes into being successful at whatever endeavor you choose.

You are not a successful insurance agent because you battled through that steep learning curve to be good at commercial insurance. Certainly it was critical that you did that, and you had to acquire those skills and all that knowledge and so forth, but you also had to BE the person that could do those things. Can you talk a little bit about some of the things that you've gone through in your life and your career, some of those transformations that you would maybe attribute some of your success to from a personal development standpoint?

Dave: When I look at the successes we've had, you know, why I'm where I am today compared to somebody that when I see them on the street I would say that they've got every tool that I do and why I'm here and they're not?

The first thing that I'd be remiss if I didn't go to first, would have to be my faith. As a Christian business owner, that is a source of strength and rejuvenation for me every day. It's an important part of my life and it kind of goes into what I would say is the next one, which is balance.

For me, there's a balance I try to achieve in my life because I don't think we can be "all work" and we certainly can't be "all play" or we don't get the bills paid.

For me, there's a few things I try to accomplish every day and that is to have a few moments for my spiritual life with some prayer time and devotional time. For balance, I try to get some sort of exercise in every day, whether it's a workout or cardiovascular. My family is incredibly important to me, so I think so far I've done a great job of keeping all that in perspective and making sure they're a top priority.

It's hard when you have your business screaming at you and as a business owner, frankly, it doesn't scream at you unless it's the bills that aren't getting paid. You don't have a boss looking over your shoulder telling you that you need to do something, so trying to maintain that balance as a business owner can be very challenging and very difficult.

To me, that's really packaging my faith and my exercise and my family and all those things together and making those a priority to get done every day. Otherwise, I know we can let the business squeeze those things out if we let it.

One of the things I focus on is the daily disciplines of the things I need to do in my business to make sure it's successful. There are staffing things I need to do every day, whether it's encourage my staff, take the time to tell my staff, "Hey I appreciate you. I love you. You guys are great." Those are things that can go unsaid for a long period of time if you don't make it part of your daily disciplines.

There's certainly marketing things that need to be done every day to generate new business. There are client retention things that need to be done every day to make sure I'm reaching out to my top clients, letting them know I'm here and willing to help. There are educational things and motivational things.

I don't think motivation is something that you can get one time and be done with; I think it's something that needs to be reoccurring and you need to continually get yourself motivated and inspired and pumped up on a daily basis.

For me, that's done several different ways. I read books, listen to tapes and cd's, listen to sermons on pod casts, do several different things to make sure I'm getting fed a little bit by somebody every day to keep me going in the right direction.

Then, I certainly like to play. I've actually gotten to a place where I've committed to a four day work week. I work Mondays and Tuesdays. I golf on Wednesdays with about 12 other guys who are almost all clients now.

They're all business owners, from a general contractor that builds custom homes that are in that $3-5 million range, two roofing contractors that own their own roofing businesses. Another contractor that does rockeries… almost all of them in the construction business now that I think about it. We all play on Wednesdays and then I'm back to work on Thursdays and Fridays.

That goes back to the balance for me, I know that I have a lot more energy and focus on those four days that I'm working because I know that's what I'm there to do. Those are some of the things I've done. I'm sure there's more, but those are the things that come to mind right away.

Eric: *That's great. Thanks for sharing all that. It sounds like you are very intentional and deliberate about incorporating all those different things into your life and I think that's very important for all of us to hear, and it's something we've consistently heard from other successful folks we've been talking to. You just have to plan. You have to plan your life and plan your business. If you don't, it just "happens", and often it doesn't happen how you'd really like it to; you have to take control of it. So thank you for sharing.*

The last couple of things I'd like to hit on briefly... You've been around the block a couple of times and like we've talked about, you've seen many successful contractors and you've seen many that have failed. Give us some gems that have some real meat to them that will help our readers, if applied, to be somebody that would get interviewed for something like this ten years from now.

Dave: Well, let's hope there's some meat on them and they're some real gems. From my perspective, I don't think what you're readers are embarking on or they're in the midst of is really any different than what I did with my business.

A business is a business and your product, their product, my product, are all different, but I think the same rules apply. So if I was to give some "must do" advice, the first thing I would say is to find a mentor, another business owner. If you're a plumbing contractor, it may be better if it's not a plumbing contractor.

I know that one of my mentors that I have spent time with and done some planning sessions with is not in the insurance industry. He offers some really keen insight into things. He looks at things differently than I do; sometimes we're so close to what we're doing that we can't see what we need to do.

So I think if you're looking for a mentor, find someone that's a successful business owner and it would probably be preferable if they're not in your same industry. That's number one.

Number two, you've got to take time to step away from your business and work on your business. So often we're spending all of our time working *in* our business that we don't work *on* our business. So that would be the second thing I would say is to set time, whether it's weekly or monthly, but no less often than once a month.

You need to set time aside where you can get away from all of it and just work on your business. By that I mean, what is your three month plan? What's your six month or twelve month plan? What's your five year plan? What are your plans? Then work backwards into those and lay out from that so you know every day what are your daily disciplines that you need to do to be a successful business. I won't even try to give you examples of that, I think that's pretty self-explanatory.

We need to be able to get up in the morning and know personal daily disciplines and business daily disciplines. What are the things I need accomplish today so that when I go home tonight I know that it was a successful day? Without a vision, without a plan, without goals, we're kidding ourselves because we really don't know when we go home at night if we really accomplished what we needed to.

You've got to plan, you've got to have goals and then you've got to work as hard as you can toward those goals. You've got to adjust sometimes and make course corrections, but how are you going to know to do that if you don't have a goal and you don't know what you're aiming at in the first place?

So, mentor, goals and I would say those are far and away the most important two things. Anything I could bring up third from there would probably be a distant third.

Eric: *Awesome. Lastly, Dave, I want to give you an opportunity here to promote your business a little bit, but I also know that you truly have a heart for helping folks, especially business owners, so tell us briefly what you bring to the table for both the guy who really is embarking on his career as a contractor, maybe is just getting started or maybe it's in its infancy. Then there's the guy who maybe has been a contractor for ten years and hasn't gotten the* *kind of service from a professional like you that he should. Talk about what you guys bring to the table for folks across that broad spectrum from a business standpoint.*

Dave: Well, in the insurance industry there are a lot of different players (and by players I mean the different insurance companies) that from year to year will put their toe in the water and say, 'You know we'd like to try insuring contractors this year.' And then next year they pull that toe out of the water and they're back out. You never really know from year to year who are the carriers that are going to be around.

From a competitive standpoint, I like to think that we have a competitive advantage that, yes, we are a Farmers agency, but we also have an appointment with one of the largest national insurance brokerages that gives us access to every single market that's out there, in addition to the Farmers insurance market, which most agents don't have access to.

From a "Can we place your risk?" perspective, we really have the best of both worlds. Now, with that being said, if you look at the newer contractor, and the newer contractor being let's say five years in the business or less, and we could probably even delineate for this to say that your average contractor that maybe has one or two employees, maybe one or two vehicles - that's probably your average size contractor. He's maybe paying $10,000 to $30,000 a year on insurance.

With most insurance brokerages, that is barely at the threshold where they will give you the time of day because they have set their criteria for service based on how much revenue these contractors generate back to their insurance brokerages.

With our agency, we are built for the small business owner,

but we have the ability to service a large one. That's really a 180 degrees from the way most of them are built today. They're built for the large client and they will maybe accommodate the smaller one, but it isn't accommodation and you will not receive the service you need.

Being built for the smaller business, which is at $50,000 in premium and below, I think it really gives us the opportunity to be a full service broker agent for those individuals because we can help them in all facets of their business. We're going to provide the service they need and we're going to provide the hand holding that's needed by a new guy that's just getting into the business that really needs a lot of direction.

We can also wrap up everything for them so that when they have an insurance issue, they're only having to deal with one person, whether that be their business insurance, their bonding, their personal lines, their auto, their home, their life - any insurance issues they have we are capable of taking care of for them, and we have great staff to do all that.

When it gets to the larger clients, that is where having access to all the different markets becomes more of an issue, as well. What will happen for a larger contractor, really the reason they will switch from one brokerage to another brokerage, is not because they can't get the best price, because a lot of these guys have access to markets, it's having the markets and also having the ability to provide the quality customer service together, and quite often that doesn't happen.

In our office, we have testimonial after testimonial from clients who when they finally find us through the process they say, 'Wow, I didn't realize how easy and convenient and simple this could be.' So we get that kind of praise from our clients, and it's real. I think it's because we care about our clients, whether you're paying $500 a year or $500,000 a year we're going to take great care of you and whatever issues you have we're going to help you get them taken care of.

Service is what separates us from the pack, but we also have the ability to place you with whatever carrier we need to so you're not going to have to compromise and pay more money to get that caliber of service, you're going to be able to get both.

Eric: *That's fantastic. Dave, tell everybody how they can reach you.*

Dave: You know, the guaranteed way to get in touch with me, because we all have those electronic leashes called Blackberries these days, would be to e-mail me. That e-mail address is dave@taylorinsurance.org. That's probably the best way and then the phone number for the office here is 800-722-1269.

Eric: *To those contractors reading this: If you have any questions or concerns or doubts about the coverages that you do have or service you're receiving, or if you're just getting started and you really need to talk with a professional and an expert that is going to make sure that you're well taken care of and well protected, I encourage you to get in contact with Dave and his wonderful staff at Taylor Insurance. Dave, thank you for spending this time with us.*

Dave: You bet, and thank you. Again, I hope that the information is of value and if anybody does have any questions, please do call or e-mail and we'd be happy to assist.

Eric: *Wonderful. Well thanks again, you take care, Dave.*

TOOLBOX

Notes from the Specialists

- Communicate expectations, throughout the project.
- Use the Internet. Have a web site, or use Facebook.
- Take high quality pictures for your portfolio.
- Buy your materials from a local lumber yard, not one of the big box stores. Build relationship with a salesman.
- Network with other professionals, like electricians, plumbers, landscape, roofers, etc.
- Read *The E Myth Revisited* by Michael Gerber, *Good to Great* by Jim Collins, and *7 Habits* by Stephen Covey.
- Know the difference between your intention and your impact. Consider hiring a coach or consultant to help.
- Develop and document the standard operating procedures for your business. Teach your employees to follow them.
- Proactively market to architects. Cultivate relationships and prove your ability to execute their designs.
- Seek out a business mentor. Ideally someone successful in another line of work, so they can advise you objectively.
- Be diligent about setting goals, and develop daily disciplines to work toward them.
- Seek and maintain balance. In addition to work, make sure you are exercising your body and spending time with family.

PART FOUR | "Finish Work"

Marketing

According to Jay Conrad Levinson in his best-selling book Guerrilla Marketing (required reading for entrepreneurs for many years), marketing is defined as every bit of contact your company has with anyone in the outside world. *Every bit of contact*, which means a lot of opportunities.

He goes on to say that marketing is the art of getting people to change their minds; or to *maintain* their mindsets if they are already inclined to do business with you. Think about it, it's really that simple. As business owners, we need to do two basic things: 1) reach potential customers and convince them that they should do business with us; and 2) keep existing customers happy and coming back. Repeat until desired amount of business is attained.

Marketing is kind of like exercise. Everybody knows that if you do the right kind consistently, you will almost certainly get results. But for some reason we let days, weeks, months and years go by without doing much of it, and the next thing you know – BAM! – you're soft, out of shape and unable to keep up with the competition.

Let's run with this exercise analogy (pun intended!). If you have ever been out of shape and started an exercise program, sticking with it for more than a week, you have no doubt experienced surprise at how quickly you start to feel better. In the first three to five days you are sore, but loving that wonderful endorphin surge you have been missing for so long.

Within two weeks your energy level starts to rise significantly. Within three weeks you start to get a serious spring in your step and actually look forward to your workouts.

After a month, you're flexing in the mirror and sporting a new "bring it on" attitude that has you expanding your vision, rewriting your goals and exuding a certain confidence that has been absent for some time. It feels really good!

The same thing can happen with your business. Perhaps you've experienced it before. One day you get out of bed and proclaim that 'This is the day.' You start to flex those marketing muscles a little bit and what do you know, it feels nice, and you see some results in a relatively short amount of time. The phone isn't exactly ringing off the hook just yet, but it's ringing. This feels good, so you decide to keep doing it. Any fears you had of marketing begin to dissipate, and new, productive habits start to form.

At this point, your confidence begins to grow, and you very clearly realize just how important – and easy, really – it is to make marketing (like exercise) a daily priority.

There are many books like the aforementioned which are dedicated entirely to marketing. This is not one of them. However, marketing is critical to the future of your business and therefore will get ample mention in this book.

Please do not take this subject lightly, as it is the lifeblood of your business. Marketing is the fuel for your engine; it doesn't matter how big and strong the engine is, if you don't fuel it, you will never hear it rumble or purr.

In this section we will start by getting introspective and taking a close look at what makes you different; what sets you apart in your market. Next we will aim at defining exactly who it is you are targeting, and from there we will look at relationships, communication, efficiency and technology.

Let's roll.

Know Your USP

Your Unique Selling Proposition (USP) is that quality about your business that gives you a competitive advantage of some kind. It is not enough to just be unique. You could drive a lifted fluorescent green truck with your business name scrolling across an electronic reader board mounted on each side of your truck, and this would certainly be unique.

While you would undoubtedly get attention and turn some heads, it is unlikely that it would equate to increased sales. In fact, it would probably hurt sales.

This is where the "S" in USP comes in. You must strive to be unique, and it's important to set yourself apart from the competition, but it should be in a way that provides a selling advantage; offering an added benefit to the consumer if they choose to buy from you.

The first thing you need to do is literally ask yourself, "What's my USP? What is different about what I offer my customers from that which is offered by my competitors?"

If you can't answer the question quickly, in other words if you don't have a very clear and written description of what your USP is, then it is likely that you probably don't have one – at least that you are aware of or have articulated.

What do I mean by that? Well, sometimes when you ask a successful business person what they did to build a great business, they will say, "To be honest, I'm not really sure. We just keep doing what we've always done, and we've seen consistent growth year after year."

Some apprenticed under great business leaders and simply applied what they learned – the *only* way they learned. It is second nature and they can no more pinpoint what they do differently than describe why they are able to walk or talk.

Others come by it instinctively. If they were pressed to analyze their business carefully they could probably identify two or three things that really set them apart. In the same way that some people seem to come out the womb shy and others socially outgoing, it seems that some folks are born with an innate aptitude and personality for sales and business.

The rest of us, the majority of us, have to seek out and pursue learning, acquire wisdom and be very disciplined in our practice and application.

So, back to what to do if you don't have or know your USP. If it's the latter, meaning you think you probably have one (because you have been quite successful) but you aren't sure what it is, then you simply need to touch base with five to ten recent satisfied customers and find out from them what makes you different. Here's a sample email you could send:

"Hi Jim and Janet. I haven't talked to you in a few [weeks, months], I hope you are doing well and enjoying your new [home, kitchen, addition]. I have a quick favor to ask. I am reading a book right now about how to grow my contracting business, and trying to follow some of the advice given, includ-

ing identifying my USP, or Unique Selling Proposition (essentially what make me different, in a competitive way, from my competitors).

My business has been pretty successful, but I'd like to continue to grow it by acquiring more great clients like you. So I thought I would pose the question to you: What are the one or two (or more) things that set me apart from the competition in your opinion? It feels a little awkward asking, but I figure it probably would be wise to find out what I did to acquire clients like you so I can do more of it!"

Obviously you can tweak and customize this however you need to for different customers based on your relationship with them. But the beauty of this is that you will not only get some sincere and valuable feedback as well as a nice shot to your ego, but it'll also serve as a client "touch". They'll be flattered to be chosen and asked for their feedback, and now they know that you are looking for more business!

Okay, so what if you are one of the majority who is pretty certain that you *do not* have a USP? In fact, many times when you land a project, rather than feeling a sense of pride at seeing a harvest from your planting (marketing), you feel like you got lucky, and you wish you could persuade that fickle Fate to pour her favor on you more often.

There are two great ways to identify and develop a USP for your business.

The first is to identify and adopt that of another successful contractor. This book and the interviews contained herein provide a great way to do that.

But wait a minute, if I copy someone's USP, is it still a USP? Well, yes and no. While it is technically not unique if you do this, it is likely still only practiced by a very small percentage of your competitors. For example, let's say you decide that your USP is going to be that all of your employees are going to wear clean, professional uniforms on job sites. Yes, there are other contractors who do this, but so few that over 99% of your customers and prospects will have never seen another like you.

The second way to find and develop a USP is to make a list of the negative stereotypes of the business (there are many, and unfortunately most of them are deserved), and identify some ways to outwardly counter one or more of them.

For example, contractors are notoriously late. They often show up later than promised, and sometimes not at all! What if you told clients that every Monday morning they could expect a detailed, printed schedule for the week, and that each time they didn't receive a schedule, or each time one of the scheduled times was missed without prior notice by phone, you would deduct $100 from their final bill? Would that be different from what they've experienced in the past? You bet it would.

Bottom line: if you are going to grow and prosper, you must be competitive. To be competitive, you must offer something different and better than what your customers can get from someone else. Define what that is, then communicate it effectively to your prospects, and you will never again have any gaps in your pipeline.

Define Your Target

W hen asked who their target market is, many contractors have loosely defined answers, at best. In truth, many will take just about anything that comes their way without giving much thought to whether it is the kind of business they can do, that they *should* be taking, or whether the client is someone they would like to work with.

Once in a while, they work on a project where it is a great fit; the work is right up their alley and they gel nicely with the client.

But all too often, work comes out of nowhere, thanks to an unsolicited referral, a mention of you or your work by a friend or client in a random conversation, or some other fortunate, but unintended circumstance. The client may not be a good personality match, and their expectations are not in line with yours, but it's work, so you take it.

Have you ever heard the expression, "You can please some of the people all of the time, and all of the people some of the time, but you can't please all of the people all of the time?"

Smart business owners know and understand this principle, and they focus their marketing efforts on the "some" that they can please "all of the time."

An extreme example of what we are talking about here is this: Let's say you design and install high-end kitchen remodels. Would it be better to mail out a professionally designed brochure to a targeted list of upper-income neighborhoods, or put flyers up on bulletin boards in apartment complexes?

The answer is obvious, even silly, but you would be surprised how often business owners give almost no thought to who they are targeting, let alone the message they are trying to communicate to that target.

Much more fulfillment—and profit—will result if you will take the time to write out a detailed description of your ideal customer. Here are some of the benefits you will realize:

- Your Reticular Activating System (RAS) will be turned on and you will recognize more opportunities that are "up your alley."
- You will be quicker to recognize opportunities which do NOT fit your target profile, and be better able to walk away from ones which would be especially ill advised.
- Your work will be of higher quality. If you are targeting people you like, who have the right expectations and means, and you are doing work for them at which you are skilled, then you can not help but enjoy your work more and produce a higher quality "product."
- Your referral sources will be better prepared to proactively refer people to you. When you communicate your target profile to your clients and referral sources, they are more likely to think of you when they hear of an opportunity, because your clear target description will be impressed upon *their* RAS.

Right now, go to your day planner and schedule some time this week to clearly define – on paper – your target customer.

Go into as much detail as possible. Describe their income, their social tendencies, the types of neighborhoods and homes in which they live, the places they work, shop and play, etc.

If you will take the time to do this, and then proactively pursue your target by focusing your marketing, your business will grow exponentially.

A final note on this subject…Arguably as important – if not more important – than knowing your target, is knowing what you are good at and admitting what you are not.

Doing work we are good at and enjoy usually leads to quality results, happy customers, and personal pride and fulfillment. Doing work which we hate or are not good at results in the exact opposite of these.

> *"Make your strengths productive and your weaknesses irrelevant."*
> *-Bob Crosetto*

Make the Right Connections

I t's not *what* you know, but rather *who* you know. That's what they say. No matter who you are, where you come from, or what you've done, you can probably think of at least a few examples that prove this.

Of course *what* we know is important, but so often in life and business, opportunities are exposed and doors are opened due to a personal relationship or introduction.

It is no different with your business. How many times have you won a project where the client didn't even get any other bids, simply because they knew you or were referred by a friend, colleague or architect they trusted? Many times, right?

We all want to make good decisions with our money that we

won't regret, and most of us do so by both soliciting and evaluating multiple bids or quotes, or by getting a referral from a trusted friend or professional. Sometimes it is both, but often a solid referral removes the client's urge to get multiple bids, and even brings them a sense of relief because the bid process can be very time- and energy-consuming.

Knowing this and if presented with the choice, would you rather bid on projects where you are one of several bidders, or be referred by a trusted source and likely to be the only bidder? The latter, of course!

In the previous section you defined your target. Your task now is to identify the people/professionals who are in a position to refer potential clients who fit your target profile. This list might include:

- Realtors
- Architects
- Accountants
- Financial Advisors
- Interior Designers
- Other contractors (who don't do what you do)

There are potentially many more that you could add to this list. Put some thought into it.

The next step is to start identifying targets within each source category. For example, if you think or have experienced that architects are a good referral source for clients who fit your profile, start by jotting down the names of any architects you know.

Also write down a few names of people you know personally who know architects (your insurance agent, your financial advisor, anyone you know who has recently built or remodeled a home, etc.). Call or email them and ask, "Do you know any good architects you'd recommend? Would you be willing to introduce me?"

Beyond this, do an internet or yellow pages search for architects in your target geographic area, listing out five or ten or twenty that you will commit to contacting.

Next step, for each contact or group (e.g. personal contact, friend referral, yellow pages) make note of whether you will contact them by phone, mail or email.

Follow the steps above for each category which you have identified for your referral source target list.

Once this is done, you need to create a rough template for each communication strategy. Create a script for the ones you will contact by phone. Write a template letter for email messages, as well as one for those you plan to contact by mail.

If you are wondering which form of communication you should use, here is my suggestion. Whenever possible, talk to someone on the phone. Leave a voice mail if you have to and keep following up til you reach them.

Second to phone, in my opinion would be to send a nicely written, hand-signed letter on letterhead. Email is extremely quick and convenient, but so easily gets buried in the inbox. Use it for follow-up to a phone call, but unless it's a personal friend, try not to make it your first contact with regard to striking up a referral relationship.

As far as what to say, whether it's on the phone or in your letter, keep it simple. Your objective is to schedule a time to meet briefly. Respect their time and tell them that you would like to take twenty minutes to learn about their business so you can be a good referral source for them. Never mind that you are looking for the same from them; go in with a "what can I do for you?" attitude and you will naturally get your own needs met.

Once you get the opportunity to meet with some of the folks you contacted (not everyone will be agreeable to a meeting), again, keep things simple and keep your focus on how you can help them. Let Zig's message play in your mind at all times. *You can have everything in life that you want, if you will help enough other people get what they want.*

After that, be sure to follow up with a thank-you note, and add them to your mailing list for your newsletter or other communications (see Stay in Touch in later section).

Architects in many cases are great referral sources for contractors, but have you ever thought about targeting real estate agents? They are mainly looking to buy and sell homes, but often their properties need repairs prior to sale.

More importantly, most realtors are social people. They are often leaders, involved in many groups and activities. And they like to be a "go to" person in their Circle of Influence.

Call a few brokers in your community and ask if you can come and make a five-minute presentation at their next sales meeting. They all meet every week, and would likely welcome you with open arms. Bring donuts and lots of business cards, and don't be surprised if your phone rings within hours.

It's all about connections. Identify people who are trusted advisors, either professionally or informally. Cultivate a relationship, and educate them on what you do and who your ideal customer is. All the while, learn about them and strive to help them. If you plant good seed in fertile ground, you will later reap a bountiful harvest.

Recruit Your Cheerleaders

This section is relatively short but extremely important. Every business, including yours, needs a few enthusiastic cheerleaders.

If you're a remodeler, you need some happy customers who aren't shy about telling their friends about your work. If you're a painter, you need the same thing, as well as a few other subcontractors who might pass your name along to a GC they are working with.

No matter what you do, it never hurts to have a few folks out there who will keep their eyes peeled for opportunities for you, and willingly offer up their recommendation.

You may already have a few people who love your work, and wouldn't hesitate to recommend it, but their radar simply hasn't been activated.

So here is what you do: Call one of these people and tell them how much you appreciate their business and/or friendship. Tell them that you are looking to grow, and that referrals are the lifeblood of your business. In a very serious and sincere tone, let them know that they are one of a few people you are contacting to see if they'd be willing to actively and consciously be on the lookout for opportunities.

Let them know how much you value their judgment, and that you recognize how other people probably put as much stock in their recommendations as you do. So you would be so grateful if they would be on the lookout, and maybe even proactively contact a few folks, because you would love to have a few more clients like them.

We're not trying to lather on phony flattery here, so make sure it truly is someone whose judgment and character you respect. But assuming so, can't you see where they *would* be flattered to be asked for your help, especially when presented in this way? You bet they would.

Set a goal to get commitment from five new cheerleaders each month. Try to pick from different circles when you can, so as to not have too much overlap.

For instance, call one friend from college, one friend from church, another from the gym, another from your softball team, and another from your kids' school.

A couple of final bits of advice that simply must be followed if you want to maximize your efforts and not shoot yourself in the foot.

First, <u>always</u> follow up the conversation with a hand-written thank you note. Express sincere thanks to the person for their commitment to help, and include five to ten business cards they can give to anyone they see fit.

Second, <u>always</u> follow up with an email or hand-written note whenever you get a referral. "Hi Joe. I just wanted to let you know that I got a call from Betty Jones about a new kitchen. She said she was referred to me by you, and I wanted to let you know how much I appreciate it!"

If you win the project, send another note, thanking Joe profusely, and include a gift card to Starbucks or a restaurant or something. It doesn't have to be a lot, but don't be chincy either; thanks to Joe you got a new client and paid some bills. The more he feels appreciated, which is a feeling we all desire, the more committed he will be to referring business again in the future.

Stay in Touch

W hat is the most important factor when it comes to making sure you are top of mind with your cheerleaders? You guessed it: staying in touch.

Think about it – which restaurants do you typically recommend to friends, the ones you ate at recently or a year ago? This isn't a perfect example because we all have favorites we go to for years, but the point is that you are much more likely to recommend something – or someone – that you have experienced, thought of, or connected with recently.

With all the competing marketing messages we receive these days, you can not expect people to remember you indefinitely. You need to keep in touch. There are many ways to do this, and I'd suggest you pick at least one of the techniques below and make it a monthly or quarterly discipline.

The first is to simply send an email. If your list is big, as in perhaps you have added all of your past clients to it or something like that, then send a broadcast email, which means it is one email sent to all the recipients (blind copied) at once.

If your list is smaller, then it would be worth taking the time to send each person a personalized email. You can copy and paste the main info into each email, but add some personal touches at the beginning and end. Sending emails is very inexpensive; the only investment is some time.

The other way to very inexpensively stay in touch is the good old telephone. Implement a daily discipline to make one "fan" call every day. Or, devote a few hours every two weeks, or once a month, to just making these calls. This warm, voice-to-voice contact will go far.

The third way to stay in touch is to mail out a monthly or quarterly newsletter. Now, this can be very effective, and extremely well received, but is more work and certainly more costly than the other two strategies above, which are free.

However, despite the cost, a well done newsletter with solid and timely information can pay for itself many times over. Not only does it accomplish the primary task of keeping you fresh in their minds, it also enhances your image as a professional; helping you stand out from the crowd.

If you are feeling a little overwhelmed right now about where to even start to develop your own newsletter, take a deep breath. You do not have to design the newsletter, nor do you have to even write anything. You don't even have to lick stamps if you don't want to!

There are companies which provide turn-key services for communicating with your past and prospective clients. They do the research, write the articles, handle the graphic design, everything. On top of that, if you provide them with your mailing list, they will print, label and ship the newsletters for you, month after month (or quarter after quarter, whichever you choose).

See the Toolbox at the end of Part IV for newsletter providers.

Hopefully you are in agreement at this point that enlisting a small army of raving fans who will raise their virtual megaphone and tell the world about you is vitally important to growing your business. Yes, you can and should do the minimum, which is produce quality work that will leave your customers satisfied and willing to give a good testimony if asked. But don't ever discount the power of igniting some proactive praise by keeping yourself fresh in the minds of your fans – and ASKING for their help. Keep the fire stoked, and your pipeline will be bursting at the seams.

Make Technology Work for You

Τhe construction industry is understandably one of the slower adopters of technology. There are some segments of the business which are highly technology dependent and have embraced the advancements. But by and large, there is quite a gap between them and much of the rest of the business world.

Here it is 2010 and you literally can still find contractors submitting hand written estimates on yellow pads, and with smudged McDonalds napkins on their dash boards containing notes from a walk-through. Tucked beneath and between those are business cards, material receipts, invoices and all sorts of other items which are important, but which get forgotten, lost and damaged.

I know that you know what I'm talking about. Do yourself and your business a favor and make technology your friend. And we're not talking about anything super advanced here.

First of all, get yourself a smart phone (like a Blackberry), and take advantage of its features. Here are just a few of the things you can do if you have a smart phone:

- Send and receive email. You'll never miss an opportunity due to only being able to check email in the late evening or early morning hours.
- Keep client and project notes organized and at your finger tips. Never again will you have to dig through

the pile on the dash board ("I know I wrote it down somewhere!")

- Keep contacts up to date and organized. No more business cards tucked in your wallet or on the dash. You can easily categorize your contacts too. Need a painter? Within seconds pull up a list of painters in your contact directory.
- Take and organize quality job-site photos and video. Take "before and after" photos for your portfolio. Visually document progress on projects. Photograph problem areas and accident scenes.
- Review – and even produce or edit – client estimates and contracts, invoices, subcontractor agreements, and more.
- Search the internet for material photos and pricing, research suppliers and contractors, google a construction technique or building code, etc.

There are many more features and benefits, but as you can see these alone could greatly improve your organization, communication and efficiency, thus increasing your capacity for business as well as for satisfying your existing clients. And all this will result in higher profit.

The next thing that will be of great benefit to you will be a professional – but not necessarily pricey – web site. It's so easy and affordable these days to produce and maintain a professional site that if you don't have one, clients are almost compelled to question your credibility.

According to Jay Conrad Levinson in Guerrilla Marketing, your web site should include these ten critical elements:

1. *An attention grabbing headline.* It's the first thing visitors see and you want it to clearly and concisely describe what you offer.

2. *User-friendly navigation.* Internet users no longer have patience for poor navigation and cumbersome location of information. You want to lose people quickly? Make your site tough to navigate.

3. *Great sales copy.* Your web site is your first, and sometimes only shot at persuading and convincing a customer that working with you is the best decision. Make sure you don't waste that shot.

4. *A clear call to action.* Don't make people guess what you want them to do. Tell them exactly what to do, and make it easy to do it.

5. *Graphics with a purpose.* Give your site "curb appeal" by using crisp, professional graphics and photos. Make your photo gallery very pleasing to the eye and make sure it highlights your best work.

6. *A strong opt-in offer.* Folks that visit your site may not be ready to move ahead with a project right now, but are just poking around. Wouldn't you love to be able to know they visited your site and keep in touch with them? Ask them to enter their name and email address so you can send them your monthly e-newsletter. Offer a free article for signing up, like "The Top 10 things every homeowner must know before starting a home project." There are dozens of free articles like this on the internet.

7. *Testimonials.* This is huge. As Levinson states, the best

way to establish credibility is to provide evidence that your product or service really works. This third party validation, even though the third party is unknown, is extremely effective, as our nature is to be fearful being the first to use a product, service or contractor.

8. *An "About Us" page.* Unless you are a huge company selling a commodity, customers would really like to know that they are dealing with real people. Especially when it comes to contractors, they are put at ease when they can see the happy smiling faces of the contractor and his employees. Tell the story of how your company was born. Talk about your mission and vision. Let your prospects and client bond with you on a personal level.

9. *A FAQ page.* If you don't know it, FAQ stands for Frequently Asked Questions. Think of the most common questions prospects have of you, or even contractors in general, and answer them. Do you get tired of people calling to see if you build decks, when all you do is kitchens and baths? Put it in your FAQ! It's a great way to save time and pre-qualify your prospects. When they call, they are informed and ready to talk about important topics.

10. *Your contact info.* Provide all means of contacting you. Include your mailing address (unless it's your home address, in which case consider getting a mailbox), your email address, phone and fax. Never leave any question at all as to how to reach you or your company.

Once you have built and launched your web site, it's important that you review and update it regularly. Make sure you are putting up new and current "before and after" photos, as well as testimonials. There's nothing quite like a long list of testimonials.

A last word on your web site, and any other marketing "materials" for that matter. Remember our conversation early on about emulating successful people? Apply that here as well.

Peruse other contractors' web sites and make note of things you like and don't like. Use these observations as guidelines when you design your own, and do the same thing with logos, flyers, brochures, business cards and anything else where your clients come into contact with you. Don't reinvent the wheel!

Go to any construction industry trade show and you will learn about all kinds of technologies available to you like estimating software, client management systems, marketing services, and more. Most have some great features and may or may not help you at your level of business.

Ultimately, you have to ask yourself, "Will this help me run my business more profitably?" And if the answer is yes, then you must determine if you can afford it, and how far out is the ROI (return on investment)? No matter what level you are at currently, the advice given in this section will help you immensely if implemented. Beyond that, evaluate advanced technologies for your business with the above questions in mind.

Remember – technology is your friend!

TOOLBOX

- **Raving Fans** by Ken Blanchard
  You must read this book if you want to have raving fans for customers. It's a classic.
- Copy writing, web design, newsletters and more:
  - **In Touch Today** www.intouchtoday.net
    Custom newsletters (print and electronic) for a variety of professions including contractors. Full mailing and database maintenance capabilities.
  - **Elance** www.elance.com
    Great site for locating and hiring freelance designers, writers, programmers and more.
  - **99 Designs** www.99designs.com
    Multiple (often dozens) of designers from all over the world compete for your business, submitting their ideas and designs for you to choose from. Very affordable and remarkably professional.
  - **Craigslist** www.craigslist.com
    Look for local designers and programmers, or place free "help wanted" ads.
- Read **Guerrilla Marketing**. Will pay for itself many times over.
- The Bridge to Profit web site will be stocked with various marketing resources. Check often for updates.

PART FIVE | "Sell It!"

See It – Believe It – Do It!

When you sit down on a chair, do you twist your body and crane your neck around to watch your backside all the way until it reaches the seat? Probably not. More likely, you approach the chair, lock in the landing pad (perhaps even in your peripheral vision), face away from the chair and sit back.

While admittedly crude, this is an example of belief. You sit back into a chair without looking because you know from many experiences with chairs that in almost every case, unless the chair is broken or there happens to be a prankster nearby, you will arrive safely on the seat of the chair and it will hold you and keep you from falling to the floor.

If it's a cushioned chair and one you know well, you may even *fall* into the chair, with great trust that no bodily harm will come from it.

The reason for this little example is to illustrate how much our actions are influenced by our beliefs. When we believe that we can do something successfully, we don't hesitate to take action.

Sometimes that belief stems from the fact that we've done it before and have every reason to believe that we can do it again. Other times it comes from seeing someone else do it, and believing that "if he can do it, I can do it."

Jim Rohn said that the first step is to imagine what's possible. The second step is to believe that what's possible is possible for *you*. The final step is to go to work and make it real.

See it in your mind; envision yourself being successful at the level you would like. Then, begin to believe that it is truly possible for you, either because you've done it before or because someone else has done it and you believe that if they can do it, you can do it.

Finally, go to work and make it real. Don't let fear stop you. Are you afraid to go after a $50,000 project because it's way bigger than anything you've done before? Well stop it. There are contractors with no more skill or ability than you who won't even think about a $50K project because it's too small.

Guess what - at some point in the past they stepped through their fear and did their first $50K project. They did the same thing when they took on their first six-figure project, and then their first seven- or eight-figure project. But they had to believe that they could do it – at each level – and then take action.

The men profiled in this book have not been successful at everything they have tried; far from it. But they never stopped believing in themselves and they kept trying, kept taking action.

And there's one more thing you should know. Every one of these men would say to your face, "If I can do it, you can do it." They don't possess some extraordinary talent or ability; they simply have a desire to grow and be successful, and the willingness to take action.

Do you have a desire to be successful? Do you believe that you can be? Are you willing to take consistent, persistent action toward that end? If so, then you WILL be every bit as successful as you want to be – but only as successful as you believe you can be.

Be a Champion

T here are lots of definitions for "champion.". The champion is most often defined as the one who has defeated all opponents in a competition so as to hold first place.

That's fine, but not what I'm talking about here. A champion in my opinion is someone who competes and wins to the extent that they are capable, and does so with integrity, such that the rewards that come with winning are justly earned and well deserved.

Zig Ziglar warns, "Don't judge your success by comparing what you have done to what others have done. Measure what you have done against what *you could have done.*"

Profound, isn't it? We have all been given different gifts and strengths, and we are called to do the best we can with them. We are not all called to run billion-dollar multi-national corporations, but we all have the capacity to be a champion in whatever we commit ourselves to.

It's an attitude, really. A belief. Not a champion today? Change your attitude right now; believe that you are a champion and immediately begin acting like one.

Thousands of successful people in history have described how they clearly "saw" themselves winning before they actually did it. Like the Olympic athlete who envisions the gold medal being placed around their neck years before they even compete, let alone make the team.

Vince Lombardi, the legendary coach of the Green Bay Packers said that "Inches make a champion." What did he mean by this? He meant that champions don't become so by throwing long bombs and breaking long runs. Those happen, but champions do the little things, over and over, that will allow them to accomplish their goals.

Losers, or those comfortable finishing in the middle of the pack, are unwilling to do this. They don't believe they can be successful or that they are able to be a champion, therefore they don't take the consistent action necessary to become one.

You ARE capable of being a champion. Believe it to your core, and act like it. Take action. Even if it's scary. Do it anyway. Acknowledge your fear, walk through it, and do it anyway. You deserve the gold medal – it's yours for the taking!

Take Action and Persist Until You Make It!

A't this point you know what you have to do. If you have applied the advice herein, you now have the following: a vision for your life and work, clear and written goals, an understanding of what successful contractors do, a list of daily disciplines for yourself and your business, an identified USP and target, an arsenal of marketing tactics to employ, a group of cheerleaders on your team, and technology implemented which helps you run and grow your business more efficiently and profitably.

Last, but not least, you have developed a belief in yourself and your abilities. You believe that you are a champion, and you act like it.

That brings us to this last section.

Albert Gray, the renowned writer and speaker, is famous for saying that "The common denominator of success – the secret of success of every man who has ever been successful – lies in the fact that he formed the habit of doing things that failures don't like to do."

So very true. He says further that "Successful men are influenced by the desire for pleasing results. Failures are influenced by the desire for pleasing methods, and are inclined to be satisfied with such results as can be obtained by doing things they like to do."

You can dream, believe, envision and fantasize all day long, but it will all be worth *Jack Squat* if you don't take action. Are you guaranteed success if you take action? No, but I guarantee you will fail if you don't. The farmer is not assured of a harvest if he plants, but he is certainly assured of going hungry if he doesn't plant.

But it's not enough to just resolve to take action. It's imperative, but not enough. You must resolve to persist.

One of Brian Tracy's Laws of Success is the Law of Persistence, which states that your ability to persist in the face of setbacks and disappointments is the measure of your belief in yourself and your ability to succeed.

In other words, the stronger your belief in yourself and your ability to succeed, the harder you will fight and press though setbacks and opposition. Because you already see yourself finishing the marathon and believe that you can, you will refuse to quit. You will press on, despite the side-aches, blisters, fatigue and pain, because you know there is a finish line and that you will reach it.

Can you see how easy it would be to submit to the pain and

quit if you didn't have a goal, and a belief that you could accomplish it?

Persistence and belief go hand in hand. The more you believe, the more you will persist. The more you persist, the stronger your belief becomes, which therefore fuels your resolve to persist!

As we come to a close, I feel compelled to share several things that are on my heart. The first is **Gratitude**. Thank you so much for making the investment in yourself by not just buying my book, but reading to this point.

The second is **Hope**. I sincerely hope that this book and the information herein has been helpful to you, and was of value far beyond the price you paid. I also hope that you and your business are wildly successful, whatever that looks like for you.

Finally, I am filled with **Optimism**. I am optimistic about the possibilities for both you and me, if we will believe in ourselves, take action, and persist. I am excited about the fruit that will come from our work if we will follow the examples of champions before us. And I am thrilled that God has a great plan for me, and that He has one for you, too!

Bridges are all around us…to profit, happiness and a wonderful life. Just take the step.

Final Thoughts with
Chris Widener

C hris Widener, *New York Times, Wall Street Journal* and Amazon.com Best-Selling author is a seasoned businessman, author and speaker. He has for nearly twenty years been involved in leadership in the business community, the non-profit world, and as a speaker and author. He has learned what he shares through his own experience and his interaction with and observation of the most successful people in the world.

Chris has shared the speaking stage with many of the best, such as Zig Ziglar, Jim Rohn and Brian Tracy, and is considered one of the premier speakers and leaders of our time.

I have been a huge fan of Chris and his work for years, and have had the distinct privilege and honor of getting to know him on a personal level. Chris is the real deal, and it is with a great amount of gratitude and humility that I present to you some words of advice and encouragement from a man as equipped as any to deliver them.

Eric: *Chris, thank you for taking the time. Please start by talking about the importance of knowing your "WHY", and the importance of clarifying your vision and purpose.*

Chris: The "knowing your why" is an interesting thing. That's a term that a lot of people use and it always reminds me of the word motivation. Every now and then people will ask 'Are you a motivational speaker?' I always kind of laugh at that because whenever I think of that I always think of that old Chris Farley skit on Saturday Night Live: *Matt Foley-Motivational Speaker.*

The term motivation, motivational, is interesting to me because I think a lot of people think that they need someone else to motivate them, and I frankly believe that we can only motivate ourselves. The reason I have come to that conclusion is because I was taught by my mother to always love words and language, which is probably a big reason why I became a writer. Anyway, she taught me to love words and to look at the root of words to understand them.

So when I started really thinking about motivation, of course the first thing you do is look at the root word and the root word is "motive". It's interesting to me because a lot of times people think of motivation as being emotion based.

You know, there's the seminars that come through town with a bunch of speakers and that kind of thing. If you tell someone you went to a motivational speaker, a motivational seminar, most people will picture a certain kind of atmosphere. Like a big rah-rah atmosphere or lots of loud music and flashing lights and loud speakers talking about it at an exciting level. It tends to be construed as something sort of emotion based.

But when you go to the dictionary and you look at the word motive, it says "a compelling reason to act". And I found that interesting because the word "reason" is more of a cognitive based word. It made me really realize that motivation is more cognitive and internal than something emotional that stems from some external stimulus.

So it really made me start thinking differently primarily between the words *motivation* and *inspiration*. Inspire means to breathe in. I always think of the CPR class we took when we were growing up, with Resuscitation Annie, where you had this body that went limp on the ground and you had to breathe into it, breathe life into it.

To me, that's what external stimulation does. I can inspire somebody else, but I can't motivate someone else, because I can breathe excitement, so to speak, on other people, but I can't come up with their compelling reason to act. Everybody individually has to come up with their own compelling reason to act.

For some people, they want to be successful because they never had money and they want to be wealthy. For other people their motivation is to provide their children with the life they never had. For others they might want to build their business so they can support ten or twenty or fifty families, and be that kind of backbone for society.

Whatever the compelling reason to act is, getting down to this WHY question; that's something each individual has to find for themselves. It's not something that someone else can give them. It's something that they have to really look deeply inside of themselves and ask "Why is it I do what I do?" Or "Why is it I need to do what it is that I want to do?"

One of the illustrations that I always give is this little story I read in Reader's Digest or Guidepost or something like that. But I read a story about a guy who was about 150 pounds overweight.

Now, everybody who is 150 pounds overweight knows *how* to lose weight. They know how to lose it. We all know how to lose weight: you eat right, you exercise, you stop consuming the sugars and starches, and you start lifting weights, etc. Everybody sort of knows the basics of the *how*. But what this guy really needed was the *why*.

As the story goes, his daughter got sick and had to go to the doctor. Long story short, the doctor told her she needed a kidney transplant. Initially they all wanted to look at the family members first, and found that the dad was the perfect match.

They brought the dad in and said we've got some good news and some bad news: the good news is you're a perfect match, the bad news is you're too fat; we can't do the surgery on you. So the dad says okay, what do I need to do and how long do I have to do it? The doctors told him he needed to lose 75-100 pounds in the next nine months, and they could do the surgery and take care of his daughter.

Of course we can all guess what happened. Dad lost the weight. Why? Well, because he finally had a motive; he finally had a compelling reason to act. It was the life of his daughter. And the life of his daughter was the very thing that made him say "I have to lose this weight." And he finally did it.

One other note that I would say on the idea of finding your why. Money is not a very good motivator. Money *can* be a good motivator but one of the things I've found about successful people is they realize that money isn't the kind of thing that makes them happy. Money can buy stuff, but it's really once you have it; it's not a driving factor. I find very, very few people who are driven by money for a long term who were actually driven by it.

It's certainly great to have money, you can do lots of things with it, but I would encourage people to think on a deeper level about what it is that drives them; what their why is. Finding your why, finding your motivation can be hard work because it requires getting to know yourself. It requires deep reflection and deep thought. It requires connecting with yourself and your innermost thoughts.

And that's why I think a lot of people just drift, because they never do the internal work that's required to find out what it is that's driving them. So I encourage people to get away, be alone, really think about life. Do some reflection and really get to that point where they know themselves and know their strengths and weaknesses. What their life has been designed for and what their purpose is.

When you make a strong connection with that, that's when you're really going to be able to wake up every day and get out of bed and know what it is that you're supposed to be doing that day and do it regardless of how you feel or regardless of what the circumstances are.

Eric: *Very wise and profound words, Chris. Now, let me ask you this: do you think that going through this process is a prerequisite to setting goals effectively? And assuming so, can you segue into some of the best advice you'd give from a goal setting standpoint?*

Chris: I certainly think that you need to know what your purpose is in life. For example, I could open a sandwich shop. I could open a little franchise or my own little shop. I could rent the space. I could buy the ovens. I could get some brochures printed up and contact the local newspaper and put a coupon in there. I could do all that; I'm technically capable of doing it.

But it has nothing to do with what my purpose is in life. Then there are some people for whom running restaurants is the purpose in life. It's what they're passionate about, it's what they love. It stems from them at the very core of their being.

Other people are journalists. Other people are painters. All of which any of us could choose to do, technically. We could go to school, we could learn the trade. But, to me it goes beyond that. The first thing you have to do is you have to know what your purpose is in life; what you're passionate about. Why you're put here on earth, to do your thing.

I could run a restaurant, but I don't want to. It doesn't come from who I am or what my purpose is in life. If I did, it would be much more difficult for me to stay impassioned about it. It would be much more difficult for me to set or achieve the goals.

I could probably even set the goals. "I'm going to sell 30 sandwiches per day, and hire two employees." Whatever the case, I could set the goals. But if they don't stem from what you're passionate about then it's going to be less likely that you're actually going to fulfill those goals. You're not going to be pursuing them with your heart. You're not going to be pursuing them passionately.

So yes, the "why" needs to come before the goal setting in order to empower it.

As far as goal setting, I don't believe there's a single best way of going about it. I think it probably has more to do with your personality type. I think that some people are more likely to sit down and write everything down and check it every day and those kinds of things. Other people are going to hold their goals much more loosely. They're able to keep them in their brains. They're much more self-motivated and able to push themselves; they don't need to look at them every day. There are people who will disagree with that, but that's come to be my belief.

I know some people that write them down and they want to

look at them every day, and the next thing you know it's been ten days or twenty days since they've looked at them. Then they feel bad and they quit because they didn't do it right. I don't believe there's a right way of doing it. I do believe that you have to know where you're going, and whether that's just burned into your brain and into your heart or written down on a piece of paper that you look at every day, that doesn't matter.

What matters to me is you know where you're going, and you know how you're going to get there. You have a game plan for it and you're executing that plan on a daily basis. So, to me I guess the overarching advice I have for goals is that they have to be big enough to excite you, but small enough that they're achievable. They have to be big enough that they're exciting, but small enough that you can actually achieve them.

Let's use that weight example again. If you say "I want to lose fifty pounds." Okay, that's great, that would be exciting. But if you say "I'm going to lose fifty pounds in two weeks," you're just setting yourself up for disaster.

On the other hand, let's say you're fifty pounds overweight and you say "I'm gong to lose three pounds in six months," well that's certainly achievable but not exciting at all! It's not a big goal. So, it has to be big enough to stretch you, but small enough to be achieved.

You can apply that whether it's kicking a bad habit or building a business. If you say "I want to grow my business," that's a general theme. Let's say you're doing a million dollars per year and have been doing that for the last five years. If you say "next year I'm going to do thirty million," that's a big idea, but it's probably not achievable. If you say you want to be doing thirty million in ten years, that's a better goal. It's still big, and it's also achievable. Big enough to excite you and small enough to achieve. Then you have to come up with the game plan for how you go from one million to thirty million.

If you're doing a million a year for the last five years, and you say that next year you want to do a million and twenty-five thousand dollars, that's not really big enough to excite anybody. It's small enough to achieve, but not really big enough to excite anybody.

To me, the best goal setting is finding that sweet spot between being big enough to excite and small enough to achieve. I've found that that overarching philosophy can be applied to any area that you want to set goals in.

Eric: *Yes, I think you're absolutely right. Something else came to mind when you were saying all that. It's a phrase that I think was coined by Jim Rohn, perhaps Tony Robbins. It goes something like, "Most people overestimate what they can do in a year, but underestimate what they can do in ten years."*

Let's move on to the next topic, Chris. Talk about the importance of mentors, or simply identifying successful people in your line of work, or people with qualities you'd like to have, and going about adopting some of those things.

Chris: I've been very lucky over the course of the years to have people who have believed in me. From the very time that I was in high school I can plot almost up until my current life the people who have believed in me. Getting around people who can be your mentors or your cheerleaders is important. You have to have people like that in your life. I'm convinced of that.

In fact I wrote an article once called Bring on the Boosters. It was about that idea of needing people in your life who will boost your career and boost your life and those kinds of things.

Whether you want to call them a mentor or a booster, or a benefactor, whatever you want to call them, it's people who are in your life, including our closest friends, who are going to be people who believe in us and can see farther down the road than us.

Sometimes it takes some looking. You may find them online, you can find them via your church, via your local chamber of commerce, or at trade associations.

There are people who are further ahead than you are. So I always encourage people to connect with those people and say "I'm wondering if I might be able to take you out for a cup of coffee or lunch and just talk to you a little bit." Pursue successful people who are further down the road than us and glean and learn from them what we can.

It's done through cultivating relationship. You don't want to impose yourself upon them. But you do want to pursue that relationship and it's not just a relationship where you take, take, take either. One of the things I realized early on in my speaking and writing career was that most of the people who wanted to connect with the bigger names in the speaking industry were basically approaching people and saying "Can you help me be like you?"

My approach was "What can I do to help you?" That's how I ended up co-writing a book with Jim Rohn and co-hosting a TV show with Zig Ziglar and some of those things. Not because I was looking for them to help me, but I was asking how I could help them, and in doing so created a professional relationship that ended up helping me in the long run.

Seeking people who are more successful than you is the best way to improve yourself and open doors for yourself. If you want to improve your marriage, you don't go to the couple that is having marriage problems; you go to the couple who has been married for fifty years. If you want to learn how to make money, you don't go to the guy standing on the side of the road holding the cardboard sign; you go to the guy who is a millionaire.

You glean from them what it takes to be successful in some particular area. Whatever it is you want to learn and be successful at, there are other people who are already doing it, and you can learn from them whether it's in a personal relationship where you can connect on the phone or email or over lunch or coffee. Or you go to a conference where people are speaking and sharing their wisdom on how to be successful in that career.

Eric: *That's great. The last point I want to hit before wrapping up, and this is in my opinion really your sweet spot, is about faith and belief. Talk about belief in yourself, and how to cultivate it if you don't have much, but then taking that to the level of moving to action and doing so persistently til you achieve your goal.*

Chris: The whole idea of believing in yourself is an interesting concept to me. Mainly because of the balance between humility and ego. There are a lot of people who say "Who are you to think that you could do that? You must have a big ego, or you must be arrogant," or whatever.

I think that some of the people, or even a lot of the people who achieve the biggest things, are not egocentric or arrogant, but actually are quite humble people.

Here's the line of reasoning behind this – I don't know that it's really belief in yourself, like 'I'm a great person and therefore I can do this!' To me that seems egocentric.

One of the things I've realized in meeting and interviewing countless people from Olympic athletes to billionaires to best-selling authors, is that the vast majority of them are humble people. Believe me, I've met a few arrogant ones as well, but most of them are humble people who have achieved extraordinary things.

After my career and meeting all the people I've met, I really don't believe in the myth of the extraordinary person. After having met all the people I have met and interacting with them, I am convinced that there are no extraordinary people; there are only ordinary people. We're all ordinary. We all have similar lives, we're all going to die someday, we all have a brain. We are what we are.

I believe that there are ordinary people who do extraordinary things. So it really doesn't come down to believing in yourself as though you have something better to offer or you're more capable than other people. I believe it comes down to believing in results that are produced from action.

I don't think there are better people, or good people and bad people, or that there are better people and worse people. I believe there are people who take action and there are people who don't.

Among those that take action I believe that there are people who take action repeatedly over the course of time and there are those who take action and then quit when they come up against obstacles.

The people I've found that become the most successful are the people who have repeatedly taken action over the long course of time. It's not that they think they're better than anyone else; it's just that they want to do it. They're driven by that motive that they found inside of themselves that then becomes the driving force for taking action each and every day.

Now, I know that we can have self-limiting beliefs. That's the flip side of believing in yourself; it's *not* believing in yourself. To put it more succinctly, there's three positions you can take about yourself: 1) I'm better than other people and therefore I am going to achieve; 2) the reverse, which says I'm worse than other people and therefore I can't achieve; or 3) the position I'm advocating which says that I'm neither better nor worse than other people, it's just a matter of what I choose to do, and then go out and do it. I'm as capable as other people, and if other people have done it, I can do it as well. Now it's just a matter of choice in whether I want to do it or not.

Do I think we ought to put good things in our mind, to inspire us and to fill our tank on a regular basis and push us along? Yes! But I've come to what I believe is sort of a unique theory about believing in yourself. Do I believe in myself? Yes, I believe in myself. But I know I'm just as capable of *not* doing it as I am of doing it. And I'm just as capable of doing it, as I am *not* doing it.

It's not that I'm better or worse than anybody else, it's a question of whether I believe I can do it, and if yes, I believe I can do it, it comes down to whether I choose to do it or not.

So, whether it's making money or entering a new field or writing a new book or losing some weight or whatever it might be, it's a matter of whether I choose to do it or not.

Eric: *It's so incredibly empowering when you put it that way! If I'm hearing you correctly, it's not necessary that we believe we can do it, it's that we believe it can be done, and we take action toward that.*

Chris: Yeah, absolutely. You know, there are going to be people reading this book and they're at a certain level in their career and in their business. They might know somebody who does ten times the amount of business that they do. Is that person ten times better than the one reading this book? No! That person has built a business that is ten times bigger. That's it! They're not inherently smarter or any of that.

They maybe have learned more knowledge that they then applied, which has built their business bigger, but the good news is that all you have to do is go out and learn the things that they've learned and apply the things that they've applied, and you can have that big of a business as well.

That's the way I look at it. I don't believe in the myth of the extraordinary person. And I think we've fallen into the trap of celebrity. It doesn't matter what field you're in, you can go to your trade association and there's always that one guy or that one lady who walks in and everybody goes "Ooh, Ahh…That person, they're the one who makes all the money" …or has the biggest business, or whatever.

That culture of personality and celebrity is in my mind completely mythological. There's nothing to say that you can't do that as well. It's just a matter of choosing to do the things that it takes.

Is there some luck involved? Certainly. There's also some obstacles to overcome. When you interview and work with successful people in whatever their chosen field, you're going to find that yes, they caught a few lucky breaks along the way. Sure they did. But they also had tremendous obstacles to overcome. I believe that everybody gets their same share of luck, and they face their same share of obstacles.

But the luck and obstacles aren't the deciding factors, because everybody experiences them. Again it comes down to what are you going to do when that door of opportunity actually opens up? And everybody gets doors of opportunity that open up from time to time. And what are you going to do when faced with that tremendous difficulty or obstacle? And all of us are faced with tremendous difficulties and obstacles from time to time.

So really, again, it comes down to choice. Not that the people who succeeded never had any obstacles. They did have obstacles, but they persisted through them and worked in spite of them and when a lot of people don't succeed it's because they give up when they face the obstacles.

Eric: *Right. I know your story, Chris, and you clearly come from having faced tremendous obstacles; you're an expert in this area. You succeeded in the face of all kinds of obstacles, especially as a youth.*

Chris: Even as an adult though. We all face obstacles. I faced them early on, and it was a matter of survival. But some people don't survive. Some people don't choose to continue to push and grow and change. They settle. But I still face obstacles every day. That's one of the things that I say all the time, is that successful people are facing obstacles all the time.

Here's a good example. Everybody looks at a guy like Donald Trump and says "Man, wouldn't it be great to have Donald Trump's money? Wouldn't it be great to have Donald Trump's real estate? Wouldn't it be great to have Donald Trump's airplanes and cars and mansions?"

All right, that's fair enough. Would you like to have the same obstacles that Donald Trump has every single day by 9:00 in the morning? Do you know what a guy like him faces every single day by the time you're done with breakfast? Again, it goes back to the fact that we sort of make this mythology out of these rich and successful people. We look at them and think how their life must be all peachy-keen. In fact, while the rewards are bigger, the obstacles are bigger.

A lot of people are sweating over making a twenty thousand per month payroll or a fifty thousand per month payroll. Can you imagine a thirty million dollar per month payroll? Or something that some of these big business barons have to be responsible for every single month? Success cuts both ways. The more successful you get, the more responsibility there is, the greater the burden of responsibility there is, the greater obstacles you face. The higher you go, the farther the fall is.

That's one of my missions, to encourage people to think big, but don't think of it with pixie dust in the air, or stars in your eyes. Understand that success is great, but with it comes bigger obstacles, challenges, responsibilities and the like.

I encourage people to do the best they can and give back to society in the best way that they can, but understand that it's tough.

Eric: *Yes. Well, to take all this full circle, it seems like you need to have some level of belief in yourself, but more importantly believe that it can be done. Whatever it is that you aspire to, believe that it can be done and then simply take the action necessary and then keep doing it until you come back around to matching up with what motivated you in the first place, and the vision that came from that.*

Chris: Yes, and you're a good example, Eric. I cannot tell you how many people have said to me "I want to write a book." It's endless [laughs], if I had forty hands I couldn't count them. In fact, if you want to do something interesting sometime, just ask somebody if they ever thought about writing a book. They'll all tell you, "Yeah, I have thought about writing a book!"

Almost everybody has thought about writing a book. And I can't tell you how many people told me they want to write a book, and between the time they tell me that and now, most of them don't.

But you and I met about a year and a half ago and you told me you wanted to write a book. The difference between you and others is that you actually started writing it. You sent me an email and asked if we could do this interview. You took action on it. There's a lot of people I know who still want to write a book, but they won't pull out the pad and paper and a pen, or open their word processing program on their computer and start writing. Really it's the only difference. Some do, and some don't.

Eric: *Thanks, Chris. And isn't so true that whether it's the thirty pounds you want to lose, or the book you want to write, just getting in that first workout or typing that first page, how quickly you get those juices flowing and think "Wow, that wasn't so bad, I can do that again." And if you do that day in and day out, the next thing you know, "Hey, I can see my abs!" Or, "I've written a book here!" It's pretty exciting.*

So, Chris, let's wrap up here. I very humbly thank you, and I am so incredibly grateful for all the help you've given me leading up to today, and for your time for this interview.

I am so grateful to have been exposed to your books and audios and teachings, which have had a significant and positive impact on my life. So, let me help you, and my readers as well. What are some of the books you've written that you would recommend?

Chris: Well, I would recommend The Art of Influence, and The Twelve Pillars, which I co-wrote with Jim Rohn.

Eric: *I would wholeheartedly agree with the Twelve Pillars, I have recommended that to so many people. The Art of Influence is terrific too. How would you suggest folks approach reading and applying that in their life?*

Chris: Well, I think everybody needs to learn how to be more influential, and how to build the kinds of relationships where they can help other people. All of my books are pretty simple and most of them are in story form so they're easy to read and understand and be touched by and to apply.

Eric: *I would have to personally add two books to that list: The Angel Inside, and of course Above All Else, the follow-up to Twelve Pillars. Those are the four books of yours that I recommend to most folks. Where's the best place for people to find and buy those books?*

Chris: www.ChrisWidener.com

Eric: *Thanks again for your time, Chris.*

Chris: Thank *you*, Eric!

Friend,
Believe that it can be done, take action, and persevere!

-Eric

Join the Monthly Mentor Program!

Dear Friend,

Business legend Lee Iacocca once said that if you aren't enrolled in "Automobile University" whenever you are in the car, you aren't really serious about improving yourself.

Learning from and emulating successful people is the most efficient path to your own success, and that's why for Bridge to Profit I sought out a variety of successful people from whose wisdom and experience you would benefit.

To help you stay connected to this "virtual mentorship" on a continual basis, I invite you to become a member of our monthly audiocast, called the **Monthly Mentor Program**.

For just over $3 per month, you will receive two fresh and information-packed audio interviews every month to listen to at home, during drive time, or while working out.

Each month we pick the brain of a top contractor from somewhere around the country, followed by a chat with a nationally acclaimed author, speaker or motivator to share his or her words of wisdom and inspiration to guide you onto your own path of personal and professional success.

There's nothing else you could invest in for less than five dollars per month which could bring such high returns. To receive the next audio, enroll at **www.bridgetoprofit.com** right now.

To your success!

-Eric

Acknowledgements

First, and honestly not just because it's the chivalrous thing to do, I must thank my wife, Kaare. Not only has she supported me (How can I help?), encouraged me (You're a great writer, you can do this!), driven me (Don't let up, finish the book!), and helped me (Let me transcribe those interviews for you.), she has believed in me; at times even more than I believed in myself. Kaare, I wish it happened more often, but when I am great, it is for you and because of you.

To Chris Widener, who responded to that first request for a meeting and has so freely given advice and encouragement along the way. Meeting Chris added fuel to my fire, and his occasional breath of inspiration kept it stoked. Thanks so much, Chris!

To Dave Taylor and Brad Decker, two of my own personal Bridges. Dave and Brad are mentors that I am privileged and honored to call dear friends, on whom I have grown to depend and rely for wisdom and guidance, not only in business, but also in life in general, including my spiritual walk. Thanks guys, for all that you do.

To all of the Champions, including the ones mentioned above, as well as Charlie Anderson, Howard Chermak, Mike Dunn, Joseph Irons, Paul Moon and Larry Sundquist, who were so willing to give their time and expertise to the development of this book. These guys are the real deal and without them this wouldn't have happened. Thank you, gentlemen, I can't begin to tell you how grateful I am.

To my parents, in-laws and family, who have cheered me on for all these years, encouraging me to pursue my dreams, even when they seemed out of reach.

To Timothy Ferriss, author of The Four Hour Workweek, who literally has no idea how much he helped me. It was his writing that got my wheels turning and led to the conception of the Bridge to Profit series and its offshoots. Tim is a rock star with a double share of brains and cojones.

To my grandmother, aka Yummy. I've been blessed beyond words by her generosity, spiritual guidance, profound wisdom and life teachings. She makes me feel unstoppable, and I love to make her proud, which she so often lovingly proclaims.

To my grandparents: Jack and Betty Whitelaw, Harry and Doris Nelson, and Elmer Rinard. Their different examples of successful living inspire and teach me, and their generosity and wise words humble and nourish me. I am so tremendously grateful for their love, guidance, support and example.

To my Uncle Jim, aka the Miracle Man. For me, like so many others, he is a true inspiration — living proof that no matter how tough your circumstances you can still press on, live happily and be a light to others.

Last, but not least, my three wonderful sons, Gunnar, Bjorn and Bergen. They may not fully understand what Dad has been up to all these months with this book thing, but they will some day. And when they read these words, I want them to know that *they* are my "why". You, my boys, inspire me to be the very best I can be at everything, but especially at being your dad, because you absolutely deserve the best. I love you!

About the Author

Eric Whitelaw is the Founder and Chief Bridge Builder of Bridge Media LLC, a company passionately devoted to the personal and professional development of sales people, entrepreneurs and individuals worldwide, primarily through the *Bridge to Profit* and *Bridge to Excellence* book series, and their affiliated Monthly Mentor Programs.

Mr. Whitelaw is an author, speaker and serial entrepreneur who has raised millions in Venture Capital and founded a number of companies spanning diverse industries including construction, golf, publishing and Internet Marketing.

He has been featured in various regional and national business publications, and enjoys speaking to groups large and small on the many opportunities, challenges and rewards of pursuing success and fulfillment in their work – inspiring and equipping them for profit and excellence.

If you are interested in having Mr. Whitelaw address your organization, or if you would like more information about our programs, please visit www.bridgetoprofit.com, or email info@bridgetoprofit.com.